THE MASTER BUILDER AND THE WORKERS

MARSHA NORBERG GANTZ

DAVID GANTZ

D1412527

OPERATION
RESCUE

The Master Builder and The Workers

By David Gantz and Marsha Norberg Gantz

Cover Design: Brennan Norberg

ABOUT THE COVER

———————————————— ⟳⟲ ————————————————

Brennan Norberg is the artist/designer of the cover. His creative inspiration has captured the heart of the message that the authors wanted to convey by sharing their story. The little girl is the daughter of one of the families that received a house from Operation Rescue, Inc. She lives high in the mountains as depicted in the background. You will meet her in the pages of this book.

The words themselves in the title of the book tell their own story: "The Master Builder" is colored in blue, signifying heaven; and the "Workers" is colored in green, signifying the earth. The success of Operation Rescue, Inc. is directly attributed to the merging of the graces of heaven and the efforts of the labors of those here on earth.

The sunrise in the background is a perfect representation of the hope that has risen in the lives of those whose lives have been forever improved by the houses they received. Brennan hopes to share this journey with you, also giving you hope for your future.

Contact Brennan here:
banorbie99@gmail.com

FOREWARD

A LETTER FROM FR. JOHN OSTROWSKI

During the past ten years as a missionary priest in El Salvador, I have had the privilege and honor of collaborating on a number of projects with various parish groups and individuals from the Cleveland area and beyond. We hold in our hearts a common call to love and serve our Lord and Savior Jesus Christ by ministering to the poor.

Seven years ago, David and Marsha Norberg Gantz, and Justin and Ellen Hunker, answered the call by founding "Operation Rescue Inc." I would like to thank and congratulate David Gantz. He has, with the unwavering support of his wife, Marsha Norberg Gantz, completed this new book. It was indeed a labor of love.

In his book David shares his call to serve the poor, and subsequently his inspiring mission experience through Operation Rescue, Inc. As I read the book, it reminded me of why I continue to serve in the mission, and why I love it. Every day is an "amazing grace". I highly recommend this book. It is the real deal. I hope and pray that those who read these pages may discover or renew their own calling to live the Gospel in a new and radical way.

Since 2014, Operation Rescue Inc. has built one hundred and twenty-five homes for the poorest families in my parish of Saint Peter Apostle, Teotepeque. Our parish is deeply grateful, first to God All-mighty for this blessing of new homes, and then to all those to have generously and prayerfully contributed to Operation Rescue Inc. Know that you are in our prayers and that your reward will be great in Heaven.

What has Operation Rescue Inc. meant to the parish of Teotepeque? For the people of the parish Operation Rescue Inc. means that 125 families will go to sleep tonight in a safe and sturdy home. In fact, the whole parish sleeps better knowing that the housing project has greatly improved the living conditions of our neighbor. They now have the peace of mind that the torrential rains will not be leaking in and the bats, insects, snakes and rodents will not be disturbing them. Their new homes are built to withstand hurricane winds and earthquakes. No longer will anyone have to fear inclement weather.

Operation Rescue Inc. also means a healthy living space to rest and recuperate after a long hot day of farm work. It means that the children's schoolbooks, clothing, and shoes will not get wet and muddy. It means a lot less sickness in the family. It means that the visitors and donors from the United States care about them and are willing to help them in their need - no strings attached.

Operation Rescue Inc. is a project that has raised up our solidarity and lifted our spirits.

For me as pastor, Operation Rescue Inc. has been the "bricks and mortar" of how the Lord hears the cry of the poor. There is always so much more work to be done, but one house, one family at a time, has made a big difference for this poor parish community. In God's name I thank and bless the authors, the donors, and their families for all their generosity far reaching generosity.

Sincerely,

Fr. John Ostrowski

DEDICATION

We would like to dedicate this book to Fr. John Ostrowski, Pastor of the parish located in Teotepeque, El Salvador. Without his dedication to Operation Rescue and willingness to orchestrate the on ground operation in El Salvador this would not have been possible. His love for the people and the knowledge of the culture allowed the project to move forward without incident. He found the workers and trained them in the building of these homes. He also used his employees, Miguel, Chepe and Rembe to oversee the construction process.

Father Johnny even had enough nerve to actually invite us to come to El Salvador for our three month stay. We have shared some wonderful times together that we will cherish for the rest of our lives. His dedication to his El Salvadoran family numbering in the thousands is truly a work of God. He has taught us so much, befriended us and cared for us in ways words cannot describe. His is and will always be our friend in Christ.

May God continue to bless all of you!
David Gantz and Marsha Norberg Gantz

AUTHOR'S NOTE

———————————— ༄ ————————————

In the spring of 2013, my husband and I had the privilege of meeting and interacting with the mountain-dwelling people of El Salvador. We quickly fell in love with them; our hearts were full of compassion and humility. This experience awakened a call that both of us had had in our hearts for many years; that is to serve God's poor.

In the spring of 2014, we returned to the same area. Our desire to serve these people evolved into a serious commitment, one that would lead to the establishment of our own charity to fulfill our dream. While we were in the infancy stages of idea sharing, we were approached by an amazing young couple who shared the same dream. We were thrilled to join with these energetic, forward-thinking Christians. Immediately, we knew that our years of experience would be complemented by their technical knowledge, energy, and enthusiastic faith.

So, on August 14, 2014, David Gantz, Marsha Norberg Gantz, and Justin and Ellen Hunker created Operation Rescue, Inc. It is a 501(c) 3 charity that is filed with our home state government and with the federal government. Here is our mission statement:

We are committed to assisting the impoverished people of El Salvador by:

- *Raising their living conditions to basic humanitarian standards.*
- *Providing shelter from the elements.*
- *Offering employment opportunities that will lead to an independent and sustainable lifestyle.*

"Whatsoever you do to the least of my brothers that you do unto me."
Matthew 25:40

Our objective was to fulfill our mission by building houses for the poorest of the poor in the twenty-six small villages in the area of Teotepeque, El Salvador. The houses we provided are made of cinder block, approximately 500 square feet, have a cement floor, and a sheet-metal roof. They are constructed with two windows and one door; all which had metal shutters for safety. There is no electricity or indoor plumbing. We simply provided shelter from harsh elements in the mountains of their impoverished country. The cost to build this 500-square-foot dwelling began at $2,000 each, but due to the increasing cost of supplies over our seven-year timeline, it has been raised to $2,500. To the average American, these houses may seem like nothing more than a small garage. But if you compare them to the average family dwelling in this inhospitable, disadvantaged environment, you can readily see how much their living standards have been improved by these houses.

Since the need was and still is so pervasive, it was difficult to know where to start, so we utilized the Obras de Caridad

(Works of Charity) Ministry to help. It is a local group made up of representatives from each of the twenty-six villages. The representative for each village is responsible for staying in contact with all the families and helps report their needs to the mother parish in the city of Teotepeque. They deal with distributing food donations, arranging for medical services, clothing needs, and more. They were helpful to us by recommending candidates they felt might meet the qualifications to receive a home. The qualifications were as follows: the family had to be one of the poorest in the village; they had to own the property on which the house was to be built; and they had to have at least one family member work on the construction of not only their house, but also the subsequent house to be built. Since so few people actually own land in the mountains, the Mayor of Teotepeque often stepped in and gifted them with a parcel of land in order to meet this requirement. The stipulation was that they could have the land as long as at least one member of the family lived in the house. Many times, if a family was living on land that they didn't own, the landowner would evict them as soon as he saw that improvements were made to his property. The resident family would have no recourse but to leave, even if that left them homeless.

As the selection process continued, the application was filed and an interview with the family was scheduled. Using standard questions pursuant to the qualifications, the interviews were conducted by a steering committee consisting of the parish pastor, Fr. John Ostrowski (a priest from the United States serving as pastor of the local El Salvadoran church), the chief engineer and church elder Miguel Esquivel, and his son, Chepe, the local administrator of the program. If David and I were available, we were also included in the interview. Relying on the information gathered and the needs of the community, each family's history was reviewed and compared to other needy families in the same area. The Obras de Caridad representatives pared down the applicants to five possible recipients. Out of these five, only two families at a time were selected to receive houses. Creed, color, or church attendance played no part in the selection process. The only consideration was their level of poverty. Since so many families were equally poor, and we needed a deciding factor, the number of children in the family made that decision for us. The families not selected were put back on the list for the next round of selections.

With the selection process completed, construction began. Operation Rescue, Inc. had two crews with two workers each. These men were paid a meager salary that was included in the cost of the house. Helping them at the worksite was, of course, at least one member of the receiving family. Each crew had a tool chest consisting of one power generator, shovels, racks, water containers, drills, hammers, levels, string, picks, scaffolding and welding equipment. One tool chest was donated by Operation Rescue, Inc. donors and the other by the St. Joseph Church Mission team from Amherst, Ohio. Each crew was responsible to get their tool chest to the work site. This was very difficult since they had no transportation of their own, the tool chest was very heavy, and the worksites were so high up in the mountains that there were no roads. Logistically, this was a huge problem because they could only gain access through the use of small, narrow and rocky trails.

The construction of one house took between fifteen to twenty-one days, depending on the weather. However, the crews got paid for eighteen days of work, no matter how long it took to complete the construction. They worked Monday through Friday and stayed at the worksite during the week, only to return home on the weekends. This type of schedule was necessary because the workers lived in various other areas of the mountains and had no transportation. Often, they had to walk two hours to get to the worksite and two hours to get back home. They would waste too many working hours getting back and forth each day. It did help that the receiving family provided food for them while they are at the worksite.

After a house was completed, members of the steering committee and, if available, Operation Rescue, Inc. board members, visited the newly constructed home, offered a blessing, and delivered a bag of beans and rice to the family who just moved into the house. Because of the rocky terrain in El Salvador, much of the land is not arable. Beans and rice are among the few food sources that are available and abundant. They become much anticipated and appreciated gifts. We also provided a lock for the door, and a battery-operated light since they had no electricity.

It has been seven years since we established Operation Rescue, Inc. and we have seen the completion of one hundred nineteen homes. During this time, every dollar we received from our generous donors has gone directly to the building of houses— 100 percent of the donations! Any and all administration and travel expenses we have incurred have been paid by the board members. Each individual donor who provided enough funds to build an entire house received a flyer that supplied pertinent information about the receiving family. The flyer included the following: the name of the family who received the home, the name of the community where it was located, pictures of the family, their original house, and their new Operation Rescue, Inc. house. We also provided a short biography of the family, explaining why they qualified for a house. We felt that having all this information gave our donors confidence that their money was being properly distributed.

We hope this gives you an idea on what Operation Rescue, Inc. accomplished. Through David's narrative, we'd love to share how and why we did it!

Marsha Norberg Gantz

ONE

"GO AND DO LIKEWISE"

In the spring of 2013, our church embarked on creating a Mission Team. We were curious, so we decided to go to the organizational meeting to see if we would be interested. We didn't know it then, but it was the first in a series of saying *yes* to this adventure. From that meeting on, we began a new path on our spiritual journey that would lead us to El Salvador. At the time, I didn't even know where El Salvador was, but soon learned it was a small country in Central America in which the Cleveland Diocese had had a presence for nearly fifty-five years.

Within about six months, our travel preparations were completed, and we were on a plane with eighteen other mission team members headed to San Salvador, El Salvador. Marsha's excitement was contagious; she was a born and raised Catholic who had longed for such a trip her whole life, and I was a convert eager to learn. One of our parish priests accompanied us and guided us through the physical, mental, and spiritual challenges of our eight-day journey.

After a two-and-a-half-hour plane ride, and a continuum of laborious custom procedures, we found ourselves in one of the most dangerous countries in the world. The United States government had sent us several emails informing us of the dangers and advised us not to travel there. We even had to register with a government office to inform them of our itinerary in the event we ran into any political or social obstacles. However, we had made a commitment to this journey and felt that we were in good hands, so we went forth confidently, but cautiously.

Since this was our first time there, we wanted to experience the culture and the history of this war-torn, poverty-stricken country. Though we were advised not to go into the large cities, due to the violence that pervaded these densely populated areas, we decided to go in a group, accompanied by a local gentleman who served as our driver and bodyguard. We learned about the El Salvadoran Civil War from 1980 to 1992, where thousands of citizens perished. We also studied the life and times of Archbishop Oscar Romero, who was a beloved advocate of the poor of his country. Sadly, he died due to a gunshot wound while at the altar serving Mass in December of 1980. He was recently canonized by the Catholic Church. Subsequently, we were introduced to Fr. Paul Schindler of La Libertad, who, as a priest, dedicated his life to all whose lives were torn apart during these years. Violence continued and spread to the University of Central America, where more people were caught up in this tragedy. The stories of their plight go on and on, much farther than these pages can take you. However, during these days of trial, violence ensued, and many city dwellers fled to the mountains for safety. They found respite there but were relegated to living in harsh conditions.

It was this mountain dwelling people that we came to serve. Although they were abjectly poor, they somehow seemed to find gratitude in their hearts. They loved their families and considered every new life that came to them a blessing from God. They were also unbelievably generous. Although they had almost nothing to offer us, they were willing to offer us half of it. The depth of their faith completely humbled us and left us unable to defend our own way of life. We had a great sense of admiration for our new friends and were deeply moved by their plight. We also felt helpless and frustrated. As we began to consider what, if anything, we could do to help meet the needs of these desperate people, we came upon the parable of the Good Samaritan in the gospel of Luke 10:25-37.

———

On one occasion an expert in the law
stood up to test Jesus.
"Teacher," he asked, "What must I do
to inherit eternal life?"
"What is written in the Law?" he replied.
"How do you read it?"
He answered: "'Love your Lord your God
with all your heart and with all your soul
and with all your mind; and love
your neighbor as yourself."
"You have answered correctly," Jesus replied.
"Do this and you will live."
But he wanted to justify himself, so he asked Jesus, "And who is my
neighbor?"
In reply, Jesus said: "A man was going down from Jerusalem to Jericho,
when he fell into the hands of robbers. They stripped him of his clothes,
beat him and went away, leaving him half dead. A priest happened to be
going down the same road, and when he saw the man, he passed by on the
other side. So, too, a Levite when he came to the place and saw him passed

3

on the other side. But a Samaritan, as he traveled, came where the man was; and when he saw him, he took pity on him. He went to him and bandaged his wounds pouring on oil and wine. Then he put the man on his own donkey, took him to an inn and took care of him. The next day he took out two silver coins and gave them to the innkeeper. 'Look after him,' he said, 'and when I return, I will reimburse you for any extra expense you may have.' "Which of these three do you think was a neighbor to the man who fell into the hands of the robbers?"
The expert in the law replied, "The one who had mercy on him."
Jesus told him, "Go and do likewise."

———

It occurred to us that we were actually living this parable on the streets of El Salvador. We saw many people that were homeless, blind, starving, and suffering with illnesses in the city we lived in and up in the mountain cantons (villages). In fact, one day on our way to church in a neighboring canton, we came across the body of a man who had been killed by a hit and run driver. His body was left in the middle of the road, in the oppressive heat, while the blood from his head injury formed a small crimson stream that flowed to a puddle in a nearby ditch. I told Marsha to stay in the truck while Fr. John ministered last rites to this unfortunate lone man. The police had been called and some passersby stayed with the man while awaiting help. We went on to church, and two hours later were on our way home on the same route. Once again, we saw the body of this poor soul, this time covered with a bed sheet, still waiting for help to arrive. Our hearts burned with compassion, but Fr. John advised us to remain in the truck. Help would eventually come, but since the perpetrator had already left the scene of the accident, there really was nothing else we could do.

Was there really nothing else we could do? Maybe there was nothing else we could do for him, but what about for others? The words from the parable, "Go and do likewise" resonated with us both immediately. We said another *yes* to God. We could surely do something for these El Salvadorans. *But what? And how? And when?*

TWO

WHERE DO WE BEGIN?

In the spring of 2014, our Mission Team at church was planning their second trip to El Salvador. Marsha and I had to arrive at a decision as to whether or not we were going to take another trip to El Salvador. This time, I did not feel as though I was being called to go because the itinerary included much of the same cultural sites that we had already seen. Since each traveler always paid their own airfare and boarding expenses, I wasn't sure I wanted to spend the time and money for something I had already done. However, Marsha viewed it differently.

She simply said, "Let's just go and see what God has in store for us?" That statement made sense to me, and I just couldn't come up with a rebuttal, so I said *yes* . . . again. Once more, we arrived in El Salvador and made our way to our accommodations at the Mission Center in Teotepeque. Most of the week was just as I expected; more of the same activities we already experienced.

However, the day before we were to leave for home, everything changed. On that day, we traveled to a remote area high in the mountains and met an elderly couple who had lived most of their adult lives in that one isolated location. They had been together for more than sixty years. The woman was now blind and disturbingly emaciated, while the man seemed a little stronger, but was also equally as thin. Since we were there with the church mission team, our goal that day was to build them a small shelter using cinder blocks for walls. The shelter that they lived in was nothing more than four upright tree branches with a wind-torn tarp pathetically serving as a roof. I had never seen that level of poverty before, and truly didn't even realize that it existed. They had absolutely no protection from the upcoming winter winds and rains that were soon to follow.

Of course, there was no flooring in this hovel. They lived on dirt, which the rains would soon turn into mud. As the men worked to build a footer and then walls, Marsha sat with another Mission Team member and the elderly woman to pray the rosary in Spanish. They were sitting in a circle about three feet apart. At this same time, some of the men lifted up the pallet used for their bed and the elderly woman cried out "Aqui vienen las ratas!" (Here come the rats!) It was a good thing that Marsha didn't understand much Spanish at that time. She could tell that something was wrong, but she just sat there until roughly twelve fat, filthy rats ran between the women who were praying the rosary. She was paralyzed by what she saw, but the elderly woman was well acquainted with her unwanted visitors and remained calm and undisturbed. I was an onlooker to the scene. I didn't move outwardly, but I did hear a voice inwardly. The voice crying out to me in my heart was the old couple saying, "Help us!" So much was going on at the moment that I didn't let this appeal move me, until later. We worked long and hard that day and completed the walls. Later that week, Fr. John arranged for a roof to be installed.

The following day, we boarded our plane and headed back to the United States. After a forty-five-minute ride home from the airport, we arrived at our home. As Marsha and I were turning into our driveway, I stopped the car and said to her, "Why is it that we have a sturdy, permanent, beautiful home and those in El Salvador live on the dirt high on a mountain? Through no fault of their own, they were born there, and we were born here." I looked directly at her and said, "We are going to build one hundred homes for the poor in El Salvador!" She looked at me and said, "OK. How are we going to do that?" I replied, "I have no idea, but we are going to do it." Having known me for several years, she learned to have confidence in my determination. So, very calmly, she said, "OK. Let's do it!"

With the decision made, we embarked on an epic adventure not knowing exactly what we were going to do, how we were going to do it, or when it would begin or end. Several years after that, we came to understand why we were able to meet our goal. We met a motivational speaker at a Bed and Breakfast Inn in Portland, Oregon. We talked about our ministry and she shared a lot of insight with us. She said that over the years she had worked with many non-profit organizations that were struggling. She explained that most of them had concentrated on the *how* to keep their charity progressing, but they had forgotten the *why* that was their primary impetus. She advised us that our charity would meet its goals as long as we still believed in why we started it. Our *why* was clearly the old couple on top of the mountain in El Salvador, who needed many things, but shelter took immediate precedence over all.

Once again, we said *yes* to God. Of course, neither of us knew the first thing about starting a non-profit organization. Nor did we know anything about building, the cost of materials, who would physically build the house, how to purchase the materials, how to get them to the worksites; the list of unknowns went on and on. Each time I would feel overburdened with our commitment, Marsha would say, "If God wants it done, He will find a way for us. Our job is simply to hold on to *why* we are doing this."

Within a few weeks, and after a lot of research, I came up with a name for our organization: Operation Rescue, Inc. The word Rescue is an acronym for **R**ebuilding **E**l **S**alvadoran **C**ommunities **U**nfairly **E**victed. After some research, I learned how to become incorporated and how to apply to the Internal Revenue Service for our 501(c) 3 status. This status affords us our non-profit organization status, meaning that any donations we receive are tax deductible to our donors. Once we met these legal requirements, we were informed that we were mandated to have a board of three members.

We only had Marsha and me. However, that very same day, a young man from our church mission team called us and asked if he could be included in our initiative. We had met Justin and knew that he was a young professional man of faith far beyond his years. We invited him to visit so we could explain the details of our project. We knew before our first visit was over that we could become a strong team. He was excited about our objective (the *what*), he was proficient with the technology we needed to begin a website (the *how*), but most of all, he shared the same passion for helping God's poor (the *why*). About a year later, he married a lovely young woman, Ellen, who was a perfect wife for him, and a perfect partner for us!

Later that evening, Marsha and I looked at each other and thought of how our requirement to have three board members was met. *Was that an accident; a coincidence?* We didn't do anything to make that happen, and yet it did. This was probably the first time we saw the evidence of what Marsha said, "If God wants it done, he will make a way for us." This was only the beginning of such unexplainable circumstances. Marsha said, "It has to be God's amazing grace. It shows up in our lives just when we need it." It was purely a gift of God since often times, we hadn't even asked for help. It was like God stepped into the middle of our circumstances and did for us what we can't do for ourselves. I guess that is why it is called "Amazing Grace." As we began to see more of these incidents, we became increasingly aware of God's participation in our immediate circumstances. We learned to see what God looks like—his actions, his providence, and his surprising gifts.

The next step in getting our ministry up and running was a little confusing. I wanted to pursue collecting donations, but Marsha didn't want to do that until we had a clear process of distributing the funds and a procedure for actually building the houses we would offer. That dilemma didn't last long. We contacted Fr. John Ostrowski, who was involved in getting that very first house completed. After discussing our plan with him, he was one-hundred percent on board. Even though Operation

Rescue, Inc. is in no way legally affiliated with the Catholic Church, Fr. John saw the potential and need for a humanitarian effort. Prior to becoming a priest, he had been a construction worker, so he knew the details of construction. He also knew the people of Teotepeque and could choose a few unemployed El Salvadoran young men to whom he could teach construction skills. He had the knowledge; they had the strength, energy, and desire to work.

In a very short time, he had a crew ready to begin. Notice how the third bullet point of our Mission Statement was already being accomplished. And, by the way, while we were making plans with Fr. John, Justin created our Go Fund Me website, and launched it unbeknownst to us. The donations ensued. We hadn't known what step to take first, but as it played out, they both happened simultaneously. *Coincidence or Amazing Grace?*

THREE

───────────── ◦◦ ─────────────

FIVE LOAVES AND TWO FISH

W e tried to maintain as high a profile as we could. All of us were excited and eager to proceed with our project. We created several marketing ideas and plans, only to find that they really didn't produce the results we wanted. As Marsha and I were praying about it, we were led to the following scripture passage:

When Jesus heard of this, he withdrew
by boat from there to a deserted
place by himself. The crowds heard
of it and followed him on foot from the towns.
When he disembarked and saw the vast throng, his heart was filled with
pity, and he cured their sick.
As evening drew on, his disciples came
to him with the suggestion,
"This is a deserted place and it is already late. Dismiss the crowds so they
may go to the villages and buy some food for themselves."
Jesus said to them, "There is no need

for them to disperse.
Give them something to eat yourselves."
'We have nothing here," they replied, "but five
loaves and a couple of fish."
"Bring them here," he said. Then he ordered
the crowds to sit down on the grass.
He took the five loaves and two fish,
looked up to heaven, blessed and broke them
and gave the loaves to the disciples, who in turn gave them to the people. All
those present ate their fill.
The fragments remaining, when gathered up, filled twelve baskets. Those
who ate were about five thousand, not counting women and children.

Matt 14:13 – 21
The Parable of the Five Loaves and Two Fish

Perhaps you have heard this scripture passage, perhaps not, but I wanted to share it with you because it is such a succinct summary of our entire experience with Operation Rescue, Inc.

2015

In 2015, we participated in our first "Fest." This is an annual event hosted each year by the Cleveland Diocese. The average number of people who attend varies each year between thirty-thousand and forty-thousand. It features booths, games, a variety of food, and music by professional, high profile Christian bands. The day begins early in the morning and ends late in the evening with a Catholic Mass under the stars. The Mass culminates in an impressive display of fireworks. The entire day is full of fun and fellowship. Operation Rescue, Inc. decided to rent a booth at this event to raise our profile in the area. Renting a booth, providing games, prizes and treats for all who came to visit our booth was a larger expense than we anticipated. Unsolicited, one of our first donors actually gave us a $900 donation to cover the cost of the booth. This young man heard we were going to the Fest and surprised us with his generosity. Since we were committed to pay for all administrative costs for our charity, the board members gladly pitched in to cover all the additional expenses. Another donor had provided us with T-shirts to sell or give away as prizes. We had brochures, business cards, and Beanie Babies to give away. The NFL in Cleveland even gave us an official helmet worn by one of the Cleveland Browns players to raffle off.

Justin and Ellen, very creatively, constructed a ball toss game that we hoped would bring in some revenue, but we stumbled a bit on whether or not we should charge for children to play the game. After some discussion, we decided to simply ask for a donation to play the game. It was a little risky because we were trying to gain money to pay for the construction of houses. At the same time, it was very clear to me that since we were doing this for God's purposes, we should let Him move the hearts of the people to decide the cost. The rest of our group wasn't sure what to do, but they accepted my leadership and it became clear that we made the right decision.

The day wore on for about fifteen hours; it was a hot, humid day, and we must have talked to thousands of people. Hundreds of children played our ball toss game, and the football helmet we raffled off was a success. By the end of the day, we were hoarse, exhausted, hungry and thirsty. The last task that needed to be done was to add up all the money we collected to see how many houses we could build. Ellen and I counted the money and found that we only had collected $1,900.00. We were stunned. After all that work and long hours in the heat, we hadn't even collected enough to cover our expenses. I sensed the disappointment in Ellen's voice when we told Justin what the amount of our meager total was. There was no need to guess what he thought. He exclaimed, "That's all?" I asked him how much he had hoped to bring in. He replied, "Ten thousand dollars!" I had also hoped for much more than we received, but we did all we could do. After all, I was the one who said we should let God move the hearts of the people to decide how much they should donate. It was a long, quiet ride home. Negative thoughts began to creep into our hearts, but they didn't last long.

Just ten days after this experience, Marsha got a call from a friend of hers. She reminded Marsha that a mutual friend of theirs had started a charitable foundation in honor of their deceased son. Despite the pain this family had to endure, they remained humble, kind and generous people. They never let bitterness overcome their faith. So, we invited them over to share our story, our goals, and the *why* in our hearts that lead us down the path we were on.

She and her husband listened, asked questions, and expressed their opinion on what we had done, and how we went about it. She glanced at her husband, and he nodded. She then wrote a check to Operation Rescue, Inc. for ten thousand dollars. That was the exact amount Justin had hoped we would get from The Fest! We were overcome by their generosity. Never in our wildest dreams would we have asked for that much.

I couldn't wait to call Justin. When I got him on the phone I asked, "How much did you hope for us to make at the Fest?" He replied, "Ten thousand dollars!" I told him that at that very moment I was looking at a check in my hand for exactly that much. There was nothing but silence on the other end of the phone, so I finally said to him, "Did you hear that?" He answered, "Yes. I just can't believe it!" Now take a moment to recall that I said to let God touch the hearts of others to determine how much they would be willing to donate. *Coincidence or Grace?* We felt that God had heard us and entered into our lives at that exact moment again. We hadn't prayed for that amount of money, but He was with us and knew what we needed. Little did we know that this was just the beginning of God's providence.

About a month later, Marsha got a call from an amazing woman from St. Rita's parish in a neighboring county about one hour from our home. We had no idea who she was, but somehow, she came across one of the brochures that we handed out at the Fest. The brochures outlined our charity, explained our Mission Statement, and listed our contact information. She was extremely interested in learning more about Operation Rescue, Inc. and invited us to her home to ask us to explain it more thoroughly. We were thrilled to share what we had done, and what we hoped to do, so we were eager to comply. When we arrived at her home, we learned that she had invited the Deacon of their church to join us. We resonated with them immediately. They both served on their parish Mission Team and had their *why* firmly engraved in their hearts. They had been ministering to El Salvador for quite some time, and they were currently looking for a new project that their parish could adopt. Since our charity met all the legal requirements, they asked if we were interested in partnering with them. Of course, our answer was a resounding "YES!" That meeting led to donations from St. Rita's that topped $6,000 before the year was over. This was just one of the amazing moments to come from St. Rita's.

2016

I have to say that 2015 was a good year, but 2016 was an unbelievable year. We spoke to everyone we knew and anyone who would listen to us about Operation Rescue, Inc. We were excited and enthusiastic, but had no idea where it would lead. Marsha's joy could not be contained so she did something she rarely has done, she talked to her friends and family about her faith. Her brother and his wife were open to our story and interested in how they could help.

Prior to that time, her brother and his wife both worked in medical technology. However, by 2016, her sister-in-law changed the direction of her professional life and turned to secondary education. She embraced the opportunity to create and teach a medical career preparation course at the local vocational school. She was enthusiastic and highly creative in her classroom.

Luckily for us, she turned that energy toward Operation Rescue, Inc. She engaged the shop teacher to help her execute her plan to build a house in El Salvador in honor of the vocational school. She understood not only what it would mean to the people of that poor country, but also what the teenagers at her school could learn from helping out a humanitarian cause. It was a brilliant idea.

The shop teacher enlisted his students to build a very large playhouse, one that a small adult could fit into (Marsha fit perfectly!). It was designed to symbolize the houses we were building in El Salvador. The model went beyond our expectations inside and out. It was placed in the lobby of the school where students, teachers, parents, guests, and really anyone who entered the building could buy a raffle ticket for one dollar. Each person who purchased a ticket could put a sticker on the house with their name on it. At the end of the school year, the school had a festive open house for the community to attend. The playhouse stood in the middle of the celebration. Just a few hours after the event started, a little over two thousand dollars had been collected—enough for an entire house to be built.

It was time to raffle off the house! A crowd gathered . . . *drum roll please!* So many people wanted the playhouse, but only one lucky person could be the winner. The principal of the school announced the winner over the PA system. Everyone clapped, but some sighed with regret that they didn't win. Immediately, the winner came up to receive his prize. You could see on his face that he was thrilled. But then, a puzzled look came over his face. He asked, "How am I ever going to get that home?" Well, I assumed that we had thought of everything, but that one detail had escaped us all. To this day, I still don't know how he got it home.

FOUR

SEED GROWING SECRETLY

Our progress for Operation Rescue, Inc. in 2016 went far beyond our individual efforts and beyond our expectations. The few ideas we had for fundraising didn't really produce any significant results. However, donations were still coming in. *Why? How?* Quite frankly, we couldn't figure it out. Marsha was praying about our next step when she stumbled upon another parable that seemed to apply to our situation. It was short, consisting of only four verses, but it was powerful and seemed to answer our current question. It is entitled *Seed Growing Secretly*.

"He [Jesus} also said, 'This is what the kingdom of God is like. A man scatters seed on the ground. Night and day, whether he sleeps or gets up, the seed sprouts and grows, though he does not know how. All by itself the soil produces grain — first the stalk, then the head, then the full kernel in the head. As soon as the grain is ripe, he puts a sickle to it, because the harvest has come.'"

Mark 4:26-29

———

This helped look deeper into our experience and understand it with a new perspective. Symbolically speaking, Marsha and I were the men who scattered the seeds. The seeds were our efforts to let others know about the poor in El Salvador and what they could do to help. The harvest was the amount of donations that we received.

In the book entitled *The Parables*, by Simon J. Kistemaker (pg. 43), it was explained like this: "God is at work in the seed's germination, its growth, development, and ripening process. The fruit is the result of the seed; the end is implicit in the beginning. The infinitely great is already active in the infinitely small."

At that, we finally understood that the donations were a testament to God working in the hearts of the donors. He moved their hearts. He enabled them to donate. Not us. We set the stage, we developed the structure, but the "harvest" was the work of God. He was in the process from the time our hearts were moved to start the charity; His great power was within each small effort we made. That revelation was not only humbling, but also relieving. It took a lot of pressure off of Marsha, Justin, Ellen, and I. Our only job was to say, "Yes, we will spread the seed."

In the spring of that year, Marsha received an invitation for us to attend a Murder Mystery Dinner, sponsored by St. Rita's Church. It was a fundraiser priced at $100 per couple. Even though we didn't know what charity they were sponsoring, we thought that since they had supported Operation Rescue, Inc. earlier, we should support whatever they felt was worth their effort. Because the event was a parody of a murder that happened at a wedding, everyone attending the event was supposed to dress up as if they were attending a wedding reception. Both Marsha and I are good sports and always up for fun, so we decided to play along.

The day of the event came; we dressed up, and headed out. Once we were on the road, I asked Marsha, "Where exactly are we going? Are we to go to the church social hall or to the community center?" She replied, "I don't know. You are driving; don't you know where we are going?" She quickly realized that response wasn't going to get her where she wanted to go, so she added, "I have my phone with me, and I can get my email. Let me reread the invitation." When she did, she realized that she hadn't noticed the attachment. She opened it up hoping only to find the location of the event, but she also found an explanation of the event. All proceeds from the event were to go to Operation Rescue, Inc. This event was for *us*, our charity! We couldn't believe our good fortune.

After the shock wore off, we mentally prepared ourselves for the evening ahead. When we arrived, we were met at the door as if we were celebrities. Our contact with St. Rita's took us around to several of our donors and introduced us. It was pure joy to be able to thank them in person. We felt incredibly humbled. Not only that, I was asked to speak to the assembly of over two hundred people. It wasn't a problem for me since in my profession I often had to do the same, with little or no preparation. The evening was so much fun; the program, the raffles, and the stories we heard and told. A few days later, we were presented with a check for the proceeds. It was a check for $15,000 to Operation Rescue, Inc.! All this happened with absolutely no effort, or even knowledge of the event. It was just that "seed growing secretly." Almost before we recovered from the dizzying success of that last event, we experienced yet another.

In August of the same year, it was time to attend the Fest again. This time, we reserved a space in a different area of the vending booths. The cost was a little more for a booth that had access to electricity. Our plan was to rent a popcorn machine to make fresh popcorn so that we could attract more people. We also offered helium balloons with our logo to any and all who visited our booth. Since we had so many friends volunteer to help us, we had enough manpower to engage in multiple activities simultaneously. Again, another long, exhausting day ending in disappointment when we totaled up what we collected—this time only $1,500. Less than the prior year, and far less than our board members donated. *How could this be?* We had invested in posters and banners with pictures of the people of El Salvador and Fr. John who was the pastor there. Our booth looked inviting with popcorn, banners, balloons, prizes, and lots of volunteers wearing our logo shirts. *What more could we do?* Another long quiet ride home, and doubts about the journey we were on. We decided not to make any judgements or decisions at that moment. We would put it to rest for a day or two and rethink our direction after we had a good night's sleep and some time to process our experience.

While still pondering our path two days later, Marsha got a phone call from a telephone number she didn't recognize with an unknown area code. With so many solicitation calls, she usually didn't answer unknown calls, but this time she did. On the other end of the line, a man gave her his name and said he had talked to her at the Fest on Sunday. He asked if she remembered him. Well, having talked to hundreds of people that day over twelve long hours she couldn't honestly say she knew who he was. But he kept talking, and eventually, she did recall the conversation. He explained that near the end of the day at the Fest, he was looking for the exit gate, but he had gone the wrong way. He ended up in front of our booth and his attention was drawn to one of the banners we had. He was a representative from St. Christopher's Church in a nearby county. He noticed Fr. John's picture on our banner and recognized him as the previous pastor of his church, and was excited at the idea of perhaps seeing Fr. John again. After talking to Marsha about Fr. John's upcoming visit to Ohio in a few months, he came up with a great idea.

He contacted several members of St. Christopher's church and they were also excited to see Fr. John again. They offered to do anything they could to help him with his missionary work. So, he arranged to host a luncheon for about 30 people at a nearby restaurant while Fr. John was in town. All he wanted Marsha to do was to get Fr. John to the luncheon on time at the appointed date. But the catch was that it had to be a surprise for Fr. John. He was not to know that there would be any more than four people there and was definitely not to know they would surprise him with a donation for Operation Rescue, Inc. Well, that may not seem like a huge task but indeed it was. Fr. John was to be in the states for only about two weeks. It was mandatory for him to attend a seminar for local priests that would last one week; he had some errands and banking he had to do; and then he had to drive from Ohio to Pennsylvania to visit his elderly parents and several of his siblings. He was on such a tight schedule that Marsha found it difficult to burden him with another obligation that seemed only like a social event with a few people. But somehow, she talked him into it, and all the plans were in motion.

On the day of the luncheon, Fr. John, Marsha and I arrived to the luncheon on time. We were led to a private room in the back of the restaurant. As Fr. John walked in, the assembly of about thirty-five people stood up and clapped for him. He was indeed surprised and humbled by such a greeting. He addressed the group and shared his joy at seeing his friends once again. But the biggest surprise was yet to come.

After lunch, Marsha and I talked about Operation Rescue, Inc. We detailed our mission statement, what we had done at that point and what we hoped to do in the future. We paid homage to all the donors we'd had in the past and hoped to have in the months to come. At that point, Marsha was presented with a large manila envelope that contained several donation checks. The host very proudly announced that the donation from the parishioners at the luncheon totaled $50,000! Marsha was thrilled and thanked everyone in the room.

She came back to our table and quietly said to me, "Wow, $15,000; that is a lot!" I said, "No, no, he said $50,000!" She could hardly breathe but uttered, "That can't be! You must have heard him wrong!" "No," I said, "You must have heard him wrong!" It was too good to be true. So, I had to ask the host to repeat the amount. He was proud to do so, "$50,000!" Marsha finally believed it. She was speechless, something I rarely found her to be.

At this point, Marsha and I asked each other, *"Why are we so astonished at what God is doing for Operation Rescue, Inc.? We had said that we realize He is at work here, why we are always caught off guard by his extraordinary generosity? Should we come to expect it? Well, let's not get greedy!"* We were so pleased at the amount we had, we thought that even if we never get another penny, we would be satisfied. That attitude was short lived.

Astonishment hit again with a phone call from Marsha's friend that gave us $10,000 after the first Fest. This time, she and her husband gave Operation Rescue, Inc. a check for $20,000. What an amazing year 2016 was, but 2017 was full of even more new experiences and surprises!

FIVE

MORE SURPRISES

Remember I told you are about Justin and his lovely fiancée who became members of our board when we first incorporated? Well, they got married in May of 2017. The celebration was bountiful; full of fun, family, friends, and food. In support of Justin and Ellen's commitment to Operation Rescue, Inc. some of Justin's relatives donated funds for a few more houses. Plus, Justin and Ellen donated all the money that they collected for their bridal dance; enough to build an additional house in their honor. It was such an unselfish gesture for a young couple!

They delayed their honeymoon for a while, but that worked well for Operation Rescue, Inc. Here's why:

August came around quickly, and once again, it was time to register our booth for another day at the Fest. Marsha and I were unable to attend for reasons that will be explained in the next chapter. But for now, I would like to share what happened at the 2017 Fest. Justin and Ellen pulled the entire event together along with our usual volunteers. Once again, the day was long and tiring, but this time there was an unexpected surprise that made our third Fest a success.

At this particular Fest, in the front of our booth, we had a display depicting our goal to keep us on target to eventually build one hundred houses. It was enhanced with pictures of the families who had already received houses to provide a good visual representation of the *why* behind our efforts. We had hoped it would give people the confidence to donate after seeing pictures of the actual people who did receive houses. Plus, we wanted them to see that Marsha, Justin, Ellen and I were people who could be trusted to use their donation for that which they intended.

We had collected various door prizes with some high-priced items that were given to us. Raffle tickets were sold to give everyone who visited the booth the opportunity to win the items. The winners were announced at the end of the day and the prizes were distributed. One of the winners asked Justin if we had enough money to keep us on target to reach our goal of funding one hundred houses. Justin told her that it looked like we were going to be about five or six thousand dollars short. She asked him to figure out the exact amount we needed because she wanted to write us a check for precisely that amount. That's right, it happened again just when we least expected it! God took what we had to offer and even though we fell short of reaching our goal, He turned it into exactly what we needed to be on track to complete our hundred houses. We were reminded of the scripture quoted in Chapter 3 detailing the story of the fishes and the loaves. This is yet another example of us doing all that we could, and God doing what we couldn't do.

We were so excited that we wanted to share our good fortune with the friends that had helped us along the way. So we scheduled a meeting with about twenty of the people who had helped thus far. During the meeting, we agreed that we were right where we needed to be for our timeline, but still needed more money to reach our ultimate goal. A great idea came from the principal of the St. Joseph Parish School. She suggested that she would work with her staff members to set a school goal of collecting $2,000 to build a house in the name of St. Joseph Elementary School.

The school had instituted a custom to allow for a Dress Down periodically during the school year. This meant that the school children could depart from the regulation of wearing their uniforms to school, and instead wear other casual clothes for special occasions. The idea was to offer a Dress Down Friday each week. If the students wanted to participate, they could bring a donation of any amount for Operation Rescue, Inc.

Just as this idea was getting underway, a dear friend of ours who worked in the St. Joseph Elementary School office, lost her battle with cancer. Everyone who knew her was grieving this great loss; she had touched so many students, teachers and residents of Amherst with her great faith and joyful spirit. We all wanted to do something in her memory, as we were so grateful for the lessons she taught us and for the smiles she shared. The idea to build a house in her memory immediately came to mind. So, the school's goal was raised from $2,000 for one house to $4,000 for two houses. The students and parents were very proactive in reaching this goal. The donations came in to us in amounts large and small; checks from parents and allowances from the students multiplied many times over. In just a few short months, St. Joseph School managed to truly live the gospel by providing two houses for the poor—one to honor the students and teachers hard work, and one to honor the memory of a good and faithful servant of the Lord.

The principal of St. Joseph School decided to go an extra

mile with her fundraising efforts. She called the principal of St. Mary's Elementary School in an adjoining city and challenged them to have their own fundraiser for our cause. St. Mary's raised over $1,000 for our cause through various projects. Once again, we were astonished by their answer to our call.

But the story of these two schools is not just about the money that was raised. It was about the fact that the hearts of all the people involved, young and old, were moved. We had made presentations to the students and faculties of both schools, explaining how poverty affected both the children and the adults in El Salvador. Somehow, our pictures and words transcended the differences between our countries. We are all children of God; all alike on the inside. Our differences are superficial; our needs are universal.

While our partners were busy during 2017 hosting our booth at the Fest and Marsha and I speaking at the two Catholic schools, we weren't the only ones working. St. Rita's Church, who hosted the Murder Mystery Fundraiser for us in 2016, had not forgotten about us. It seemed as though our appearance at the first fundraiser spiked a renewed interest in Operation Rescue, Inc. During May of that same year, several individuals from that parish donated enough funds for an entire house on their own. This generated more than $14,000 of additional revenue for us. Again, this happened without any knowledge or efforts of our own. The seeds were growing secretly.

Later that year, we found that God's providence can be found in the most unexpected places. In December, Marsha and I had been asked to speak at a retreat at the Grafton Correctional Institution for men in Ohio. A group of Christian volunteers had been hosting weekly meetings based on various methods of prayer. In the past we visited that site a number of times, but this time, each of us was asked to present our own personal witness. While I was preparing my talk, I took time to contemplate the concept of different types of prisons: physical, psychological and mental. The residents of the Correctional Institution were imprisoned by guards, thick walls, and barbed wire. Many of us have been imprisoned by drugs, alcohol, depression, physical limitations, poverty—the list goes on and on. I shared with them the story of my personal, psychological imprisonment, and just how God had walked with me during those days. Weakened by fear and desperation, God was by my side giving me strength to carry on.

After the formal presentation, we broke up into smaller groups with the residents for open discussion. It was amazing to sit there and listen to the stories that these men voluntarily shared. They spoke of emotional pain, sadness, guilt, remorse and the dilemma of forgiveness and punishment. For many of them, their time apart from society led to not only an understanding of the reasons for past behaviors but also a lifestyle of repentance and a plea for forgiveness. One of the men who had found healing in the prison environment even said, "I had to come to prison to find freedom."

You may be wondering why I would recount this story at this time. Well, there are two reasons. First of all, I mentioned the prison of poverty. This type of poverty resonated with the situation we found in the mountains of El Salvador. There, we uncovered debilitating, abject poverty. It was poverty that was pervasive both physically and psychologically; poverty that precluded hope and extinguished the slightest vision for a brighter future. These Salvadorans felt like they were sentenced to live in fear and squalor in the mountains with no possible reprieve. Likewise, here in the United States, some of the same frustrations and obstacles led these Grafton residents down the path that ended in imprisonment. Given the same situation, the people of Teotepeque turned to their church for help. The men at our retreat were finally turning away from their addictions, crimes, and desperation and turning to God help to set them free—at least psychologically and spiritually. We had seen God's help in Teotepeque, and we were seeing it then in the stark, bare, cold meeting room, surrounded by guards and alarms. These barriers stopped the men from escaping, but they could not stop God from entering. We saw God's loving presence in Teotepeque, and we saw it in Grafton; different surroundings, same God.

The second reason why I bring up this topic up is because it came with yet another surprise for us. One of the volunteers ministering at this meeting was a friend of ours who lived in the same city that we did. We had only a moment to exchange pleasantries before the meeting began. At the end of the two-hour gathering, we began filing out, following some of the many rules of protocol that we promised we would do. Just then, our friend asked us how Operation Rescue Inc. was doing. In just a few sentences, we summed up where we were in our journey. With no hesitation, he asked us to stop by his place of work the next day because he would like to make a donation. We were thrilled as always to receive any help no matter the size or denomination. So, we complied and picked up an envelope he had waiting for us on his desk. We were so grateful when we opened the envelope and found a check for $5,000! Again, we did nothing to warrant this gift. All we did was say *yes* to the invitation to speak at the correctional institution, and it resulted in the ability to build two more houses. It felt like God was saying "Thank you" for the efforts to minister to these men, who regardless of their actions, they still deserved His love. They were in need of help, just like His children in El Salvador, and we were going there to help them. They brought to mind a phrase that Marsha always says, "Every saint has a past, and every sinner has a future."

I cannot leave this part of the story without sharing the last surprise that we were given at the next meeting. As I mentioned earlier, I had given a witness regarding my own "psychological prison." In that talk, I referenced the song, "Be Not Afraid," by Robert Dufford, SJ. I first heard that song at a pivotal point of transition in my spiritual journey. It was important to me then and has been ever since.

Well, as a surprise to me, after that meeting the residents got together on their own time and practiced that song so they could sing and play it for me at the next meeting. Of course, I didn't know that was happening, so when the quartet came to the front of the gathering and dedicated the song to me, I was shocked and humbled. As they sang and played the guitar, my heart melted, and tears flowed down my cheeks. I have never heard it delivered with such tenderness, love, and compassion in my life. This act of kindness spoke volumes to me reflecting the changes these men had undergone at the correctional institution. It was a moment I shall cherish forevermore. Perhaps, you too have had moments like this one. If so, recall it, ponder it, and thank the Lord for it. If not, be on the lookout, your moment may be right around the corner.

SIX

─────────── ૦૦ ───────────

SOLIDARITY WITH THE POOR – WEEK ONE

During our initial trips to Teotepeque, we quickly learned to love and respect these impoverished people. Every time we visited, we returned home with a degree of incompleteness. There was so much to do there, and we were only doing a small part. The concept of "solidarity with the poor" kept creeping into our minds and our hearts. Each time we returned home from our visits, we felt that on some small level we had abandoned our new friends to the plight of poverty. We had virtually everything we ever wanted; they barely had what they desperately needed. *How could we balance these two worlds we were living in?*

Well, in God's usual fashion, our question was answered. We remembered that during our first visit to El Salvador, Fr. John mentioned the fact that there was a program sponsored by the Cleveland Diocese for lay missionary couples to serve in El Salvador for a period of three years. Due to our age and my medical issues, we decided that three years would not work for us. We looked into a shorter stay, but it was not available. However, the idea stayed alive in the back of our minds. It remained in Fr. John's mind also, because in the spring of 2016, Fr. John asked Marsha and me if we would consider coming to Teotepeque for a three-month visit. Marsha's heart leapt for joy at the thought, although in the moment, she did not say anything to me. She didn't know that my heart did the same thing. As soon we had a chance to speak to each other privately about this idea; we exchanged only a few words. We looked at each other and almost simultaneously we said, "You know we are going, don't you?" And then our simultaneous response, "Absolutely!" It was gratifying to know that, although we don't always agree on everything, this path was so fundamental to the direction we both wanted to take in our retirement; it seemed like an affirmation of our lives together. After a lot of planning and logistics, we began our adventure on June 1, 2017. Here is a brief description of what we found there.

Day 1

We arrived at the San Salvador airport early on June 1. We were greeted by Rembe (who was employed by Fr. John as a driver) and his friend Luis. Neither of them knew a word of English but the sparkle in their eyes and the smiles on their faces warmly welcomed us. Their enthusiasm made it very easy for us to single them out of the crowd of locals who were all gathered in one area designated to pick up travelers. Hugs were the appropriate order of greeting and "muchas gracias" (thank you very much) was exchanged between us several times. Rembe went to get the truck and Luis waited with us to reclaim our luggage. Here we were, two Americans standing in one of the most dangerous cities in the world, unable to speak the indigenous language, surrounded by those who could not speak ours, and yet completely unafraid: We knew God was with us.

As we embarked on the hour-long drive up the mountain to

the city of Teotepeque, we began to understand why we were called to be there. As we thought back to the first time we took this trip, the scenery looked frightening and alien to us; buildings were in disrepair, vacant, and tumbling down; refuse was blowing through the streets; the people looked distracted, hungry and hopeless. This time the same scenery seemed to be transformed; we noticed the women of the households cooking in the front yards, children were laughing and playing with one another; the men walking in the streets smiled and waved to us. It was an incredible difference. *But what caused the change?* It was neither the people nor the neighborhood. What changed were our hearts and our compassion; we were now looking through the eyes of love and everything looked beautiful to us.

When we arrived at the rectory where we were staying, we were greeted with welcoming signs and hugs. Fortunately, we were allowed to stay in the only room in the house that had a window air conditioning unit. We each had a single bed to sleep in, complete with pillows and blankets. One wall in our room was a place of honor displaying pictures of the four women missionaries who were martyred in the civil revolution thirty-seven years prior. Next to those pictures was a sketch of the now Saint John Paul II being hugged by Jesus. On another wall, hung a picture of the now Beatified Oscar Romero the Archbishop of San Salvador. Above the head of my bed a huge wooden rosary was displayed. I felt as though I would surely be protected while I slept. Marsha and I both had a sense that we had come *home*; all was good, all had meaning. What may have looked like a small crowded little room to some felt to us like a haven where we felt God's love and presence all around us.

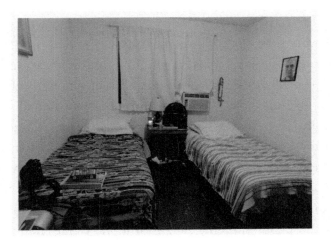

Day 2

We began the day with a delicious breakfast and fresh-brewed coffee that the housekeeper had prepared for us. Her name was Dalia; she did not speak any English, but we suspected that she understood more we than she was willing to admit. After our meal, we were feeling rested, comfortable, and adventuresome. Fr. John had gone off to one of the villages and we were told that it was not safe for us to leave the gated church grounds without a local chaperone. However, we were able to access a terrace located on the top level of the rectory. This particular building was located high up the mountain. From that vantage point we were able see across the valley over to the next mountain. Our altitude was such that often times, clouds would form in the valley below us. On a clear day, we could see the ocean miles away. Looking down, the terrain looked vibrant and lush, peaceful and calm. We later found out that once we began to engage with the culture on the ground, things could be quite the opposite.

While on the terrace, after we read our morning scriptures, we began thinking about the difficult circumstances the families in El Salvador had to endure. We remembered an experience we had on our first visit to the area in 2013. We were delivering rice and beans to the poor and met a young woman named Erika. She and her three-year-old daughter lived with her mother. The American doctor that was with us noticed a large lump on Erika's neck. He immediately made arrangements for her to get medical help. We did not hear anything else about Erika until we returned to El Salvador almost exactly one year later in 2014. We inquired about her health and found that she had just died the day before we arrived. The funeral would be the following day. Because there is no official embalming process, and the heat of the day was so intense, the funeral had to be held as soon as possible. Of course, all of us who had met Erika wanted to attend.

Like many local customs, the burial process was different from ours, but grief is a universal condition suffered by people all over the world. Not only did we want to attend, but also, somehow, we understood that our presence brought comfort to the family. When we arrived at the mother's home where the wake was being held, we were ushered passed the other guests up to the front row. We realized that the family felt proud that we were there to grieve with them. On the other hand, we felt honored but humbled to share this very heartbreaking moment with the family. After the eulogy, several people joined together to form a procession from the house to the cemetery. As we accompanied Erika's body through the town, many other townspeople joined in the very solemn procession. The group grew and grew at every turn; men, women, and children we praying, crying, chanting, or silently walking along together in solidarity with one another.

Walking along with this group was very difficult. There was so much emotional pain and sadness, and the entire town was in mourning. But when we reached the cemetery, I experienced something I never thought I would or could do. Erika's casket was placed in a deep grave. We were all silent at that moment, while most, not all, of the people formed a line. And one by one, each person individually took the shovel, filled it with dirt and poured the dirt onto the casket. The parents and relatives were first in line. It was especially hard for the first people in the line because the top of the casket had a glass window in it so that the onlookers could see the face of the person who died. I did join in that part of the ceremony, but Marsha could not. I understood, as it was difficult for me to look at the face of Erika in the casket. I share this story because it was an important part of "solidarity with the poor."

Day 3

The next day we had breakfast with Fr. John around 7 a.m. A meeting was scheduled with the Obras de Caridad. Upon arriving at the meeting site, we found that the room was filled with representatives of twenty-three cantons (villages). Many familiar faces from the last few years were present but clearly, we were the center of attention. There were roughly forty people present, including Fr. John, Chepe, Marsha and I. (Chepe was Fr. John's administrative assistant who was empowered to support our Operation Rescue, Inc. project). We were all there to discuss the current condition of the cantons. Each canton representative would be called upon to come forward and address the council members updating them on the problems and concerns they were currently facing. It was an open exchange, one that provided each representative an opportunity to be heard. It was very important to give these men and women a voice. They so often struggled with the feeling of being overlooked in society and possessing no value of their own. This forum gave them the credibility, dignity and respect that they deserved.

Of course, the meeting was all in Spanish, so we were not able to understand all that was said. But the one word we heard over and over was "lamina." This referred to the thin metal material that they used for roofing and siding for their houses. "Lamina" was the only thing that stood between their families and the outside elements. Operation Rescue, Inc. utilized heavy duty lamina for roofs that would last twenty to twenty-five years for the houses we built. At the same time, the mayor of the cantons was responsible for procuring lamina for those in need of new roofs but not necessarily new houses. The lamina that the mayor provided was of poor quality and only lasted four to five years. Even so, this lamina was in such great demand that obtaining it had become difficult and a matter of politics. Those who were close to the mayor were able to receive lamina. They often received more than they needed and would sell their excess for profit.

Many of the people of the cantons did not have a reliable source of income, so they did not have money to buy the lamina they needed. These people had become the forgotten ones. They were not poor enough to receive an Operation Rescue, Inc. house with sturdy lamina, but they were too poor to purchase their own lamina. The ministers of Obras de Caridad did not want to appear ungrateful for the houses provided by Operation Rescue, Inc., but these people, who spent their lives looking after the poorest of the poor, still had to live with rusty roofs full of holes. That meant that when the rains came, and they do come in June, July, and August, their houses get flooded with water ruining what few possessions they have. They also needed help with their living conditions.

At this point, Marsha and I had begun to understand a little more Spanish, and we heard their cry for help. Fr. John's main

missionary role was to administer the sacraments and nurture
the spiritual needs of the people. He was never given a budget
to meet humanitarian needs. He would have if he could have,
but that was outside of his responsibility. *But was it outside of our
responsibility? After all, three years earlier we heard God's call to build
homes for the poorest of the poor. Were we now hearing a call to serve these
people also, and provide them with what they needed for their houses? If we
only provided the roofing material and not an entire house, would we be
acting in accordance with our mission statement and our promise to our
donors? Should we consider helping these people?*

After a very brief discussion, the answer became clear,
another simultaneous "Yes"! This was in accordance with what
we originally set out to accomplish. I approached Fr. John
during the meeting, and announced to him that Operation
Rescue, Inc. would provide lamina for this larger segment of
the population. When he translated our offer into Spanish, the
smiles and applause we received affirmed that we had done the
right thing.

Much had to be accomplished before the next council
meeting scheduled for a month later. I was sure we would be
able to organize the distribution of lamina, but wasn't sure
where would the money come from. All the money we had, had
been committed to building houses, and we were accountable
to each donor for a house. *Where would we get the money?*

After the morning meeting, we went back to the rectory,
had lunch and rested up for the celebration scheduled for that
evening. It was the commemoration of the forty days following
Easter, known as Pentecost recalling the time when the Holy
Spirit descended upon the followers of Christ. The church was
decorated in beautiful colors, banners, and balloons while local
musicians played songs of praise giving joy and inspiration to
everyone who attended. The church was packed on that
Saturday night, while men, women, children, grandchildren,

parents, aunts and uncles all gathered together for a common cause, which is to pay respect to their Lord. It will forever remain in my heart as a holy day of great impact. After mass, the festivities continued well into the night with words of hope, gratitude, and love.

Day 5

This day, like all days, began at sunrise. The morning was spent creating an inventory spreadsheet for Fr. John. Since many of the area residents came to him for a variety of needs, he stored items such as shoes, clothing, toothpaste, soap, small tools, and more. We felt it would be easier for him to distribute these items if they were categorized and recorded.

Later in the afternoon, we traveled with Fr. John to a town named Mizata, where he was scheduled to offer Mass. We were looking forward to seeing the church there because a few years earlier when we visited El Salvador with our church mission team, we were part of the group that repainted the entire church. It was gratifying to see how much the parishioners enhanced what we had started and made it a personal place of worship for the people of their town.

In preparation for our trek from Teotepeque to Mizata, we stocked the pick-up truck with all the necessities of hosting a mass and lots of bottled water. The water is unpurified in El Salvador and so full of parasites and bacteria that our systems cannot tolerate ingesting it. It was unbelievably hard for us to remember not to ever let water touch our mouths; if one did, it would cause a painful infection in the intestines. We had to be aware of that when we brushed our teeth, rinsed our mouth, took a shower, prepared food or coffee, and especially when we needed just to take a sip of water in the intense heat. Marsha had a little more trouble catching on than I did. When she was brushing her teeth, she inadvertently put her toothbrush under the runner water. Each time she had to throw the tooth brush away. She went through three toothbrushes in the first few days we were there. Luckily, we brought extras for the trip. Eventually, she got the hang of it.

The church itself was a little more than one-half hour away with the first twenty minutes of the trip on paved roads and the last fifteen minutes on a one lane rocky path up the mountain and down towards the ocean. Along the way, we stopped to pick up a family with a baby that was to be baptized at the Mass. Mom, dad, and baby crowded into the cab of the truck with Marsha. The baby was a nine-month-old boy who seemed to be struggling to breathe. You could hear his gasps for breath and sense his overall lethargy. The mother said that he had not done anything other than eat and sleep, and had been that way since birth; he was not her first child so she was well aware that he had a problem. With the medical care scarce and of poor quality, she wanted to be sure he was baptized in the event that he would succumb to his illness.

Fr. John explained to them that he had made arrangements for the mission nurse to travel with them the very next day to a hospital in San Salvador, the capital city several miles away. They had tried to see the doctor on their own previously but were denied, and their trip was in vain. But this time, with the nurse to accompany them, she would make sure they were able to be seen by the doctor. Even though they had an appointment, it was still on a first come, first serve basis. So, they would have to leave Teotepeque at 4 a.m. and arrive in the city by 5 a.m. to begin the waiting process. Fr. John gave them some money to use for food while they were traveling to ease some of their difficulties. The next day would be long and arduous, not without obstacles, but filled with hope for their child.

We arrived at the church a few minutes late but found it full of willing participants. The church had a front door and two small side doors. No windows and no fans. The temperature was in the mid-nineties and humidity was very high. The air was thick and sticky; it was hard to breathe. But it was our home for the next two hours so we tried to enjoy the surroundings as best we could. There were about seventy people who attended mass that day; only about ten men and sixty women and children. I asked Fr. John why the discrepancy in gender numbers. He explained that Mizata was one of the more upscale communities. Most of the men whose families lived there were actually working in the United States. They would earn money there and send it back to El Salvador for their families to live on. It was sanctioned by the government because they levied high taxes on the money that the men sent home. Those tax dollars went to the government; it remains a mystery to whom the money was given and for what purpose it was used.

Now, you may be aware that the Catholic Mass is structurally the same all over the world. The readings are the same, the hymns are the same, and the distribution of the Eucharist (communion) is always present. You can go to Mass anywhere in the world and, save for the language difference, you can feel at home and enjoy the benefits of the ceremony and the grace of the sacrament. You do need to know that in the Catholic tradition, Mass should be attended every Sunday. However, in the mountains of El Salvador with a shortage of priests, Mass is often only available to the people once a month. Since it is regarded as a joyful occasion, rather than an obligation, the Mass experience in El Salvador seemed to have some delightful amenities. At least, Marsha and I thought of them as amenities. By this I mean that the spirit of a true celebration was pervasive before, during, and after Mass. The teenagers usually congregated on the steps of the church well before Mass started. It was reminiscent of a social event for them. The small children were allowed the freedom to walk around during Mass and greet anyone they might find friendly. Women were nursing their babies, and everyone was welcome to walk over to the door of the church at any time where drinking water was available. Music was loud and voices were lifted in praise, hands were clapping, and feet moved to the beat of the music. We loved it! But for us, the most amusing part was when the stray dogs, and occasional free-range chickens, would walk in the church, and sometimes up on the altar. These animals might have been unacceptable to someone from a different culture, but here, in this setting, all lives were created by God and welcome to celebrate their savior.

The festivities did not end with the final doxology. By then, the women were outside making *pupusas* on an open fire. These were corn tortillas filled with a bean mixture. Everyone loved them and enjoyed "breaking bread" together. Of course, Marsha and I couldn't eat any, but we still enjoyed the camaraderie. After the two-hour event, we got back into the pick-up truck and headed for the rectory.

We arrived at the rectory about 8:00pm and realized that our day was not yet over. Jaimie, the nurse that was going to accompany the family to see a doctor in San Salvador, requested to meet with Fr. John when he returned home. He invited us to attend the meeting with this very amazing young woman. Of course, we were happy to do so. We hadn't had dinner yet, so Dalia, the housekeeper/cook had prepared four hamburgers for us all to enjoy together before she left at 5:00pm. So, remembering not to use the local water, Marsha heated up our meal and we settled down for a dinner meeting.

Our dinner conversation centered on Jaimie's nursing career. She received a nursing degree in San Salvador but that did not guarantee that she would get a nursing position. In fact, although Jaimie lived in Teotepeque, she had been volunteering to work in a hospital in San Salvador for nearly two months. The following day, she needed to be at the hospital and begin her shift at 7 a.m. and work a twenty-four-hour shift, non-stop. She would be responsible for eighteen patients while on duty. Don't forget, she was a volunteer, not receiving any compensation. There were two nursing positions available and eight nursing students were vying for those positions. It is not unusual for this volunteer status to continue for several months with no compensation and no guarantee of future employment. This is allowed by the government and is part of how their socialized medicine system survives. While she was working at the hospital, she said, "There are no sponges, bandages, cotton balls, or other routine medical supplies." Food at the hospital is very expensive so she had to bring her own food. So many of what we regard as routine systems did not exist in the socialized medicine program in El Salvador.

We learned a lot that day; some good, some bad. Some things were uplifting, some things disheartening. In contrast to the beautiful vista we experienced on the terrace of the rectory, all was not what it seemed. Later in the week we found out that the little boy only had a slight case of asthma and would be fine with proper medication. We also learned that Jaime did not get the job.

Day 7

We were committed to help out at the parish wherever we could. But that meant finding out what was happening at the parish on all levels. So, we attended a meeting with Chepe (Fr. John's assistant) and Cesar (an English speaking member of the school staff). Cesar also filled the position at the academy as the English Teacher.

· · ·

Here is a summary of the needed projects and their cost:

- **Food** – in Teotepeque and La Pedrera (another city in El Salvador) Funded by St. Barnabas Catholic Church in Northfield, Ohio with annual budget of $20,000.
- **Ambulance** – Funded by St. Albert the Great from North Royalton, Ohio with annual budget of $20,000.
- **Free Clinic** – building a clinic at the church funded by Divine Word in Kirtland, Ohio with a budget of $15,000.
- **Water** – purified water for four areas funded by St. Albert the Great church with a budget of $5,000 for each area; a total of $20,000.
- **Academy** – funded by St. Barnabas Catholic Church, St. Albert's, St. Rita Catholic Church in Solon, Ohio and St. Joseph Church in Amherst Ohio with a variable annual budget of $10,000.
- **Scholarships** – Ten Scholarships annually funded by St. Christopher Catholic Church in Rocky River, Ohio, Church of the Holy Angels in Chagrin Falls, Ohio, St. Barnabas', and St. Rita's churches with an annual budget of $20,000.
- **New Houses** – Goal of 100+ houses funded by Operation Rescue, Inc.
- **My New Life Style** – youth job program funded by St. Barnabas' church with a budget of $2,000.
- **Helping Orphans** – assisting when a need is found with $1,500.

- **Works of Charity (Obras de Caridad)** –
  distribution of beans and rice when needed with an
  annual budget of $2.000.
- **Total Annual Budget** = $155,000

There was a lot going on for a lot of money. But the need was
ever present and on many levels. Marsha and I were primarily
concerned with providing shelter from the elements–Operation
Rescue, Inc. It was hard to see the scope of need in this country, but it was important to humbly admit that we were only a
small piece of a large puzzle. We couldn't do everything, but we
could do something. That is an important point. We couldn't be
paralyzed by the extent of the need; so we picked something to
do, and tried do that one thing the best that we could.

SEVEN

SOLIDARITY WITH THE POOR - WEEK TWO

Day 9

Marsha woke me up around 3:00 am and said that she was not feeling well. She had been experiencing some problems before we left for El Salvador and hadn't really gotten over them. The night brought discomfort and while she was able to get some sleep, it was obvious that something was wrong. Marsha is a strong woman and I must be careful to respect her as my wife, but I had also promised her children that I would take care of her. At breakfast, while Marsha was getting a shower, Fr. John asked me if we were going to join him that day on the two planned masses he had scheduled outside of Teotepeque. I was torn between being respectful of Marsha's privacy and yet true to the promises I had made to her children. I didn't go into all the specifics, but Fr. John immediately sprang into action and before we could even say "no," we were on the way to a clinic in La Libertad about forty-five minutes away. Rembe was our driver, and we also picked up a young man named Bryan who was able to speak English and act as our interpreter. Marsha was very uncomfortable, but she knew it was the right thing to do.

When we did arrive, there were nearly forty women and children waiting to be seen. Fr. John had called ahead, and they had agreed to take Marsha in as soon as we arrived. Marsha felt embarrassed to be taken in before the others, but that did not seem to cause a problem for anyone. With the help of Bryan, she was able to communicate with the doctor. Following an uncomfortable examination and the results of lab work, we were informed that everything would be fine as soon as she was able to take the medication prescribed. We picked up the medication on the way home and were relieved that with a little time, all would be well. I don't know what we would have done without Fr. John, Rembe our driver, and Bryan our interpreter. We arrived back at the rectory and were able to relax after a stressful afternoon.

Later that evening, we created a rare opportunity while residing in El Salvador. I was able to connect to the internet and access the Cleveland Cavaliers playoff game against the Golden State Warriors. We had brought Fr. John a Cavaliers' cap from Cleveland and he was eager to wear it. You should know that Father John is 6 feet 7 inches and played a lot of basketball prior to entering the seminary. We projected the game from my computer onto a large screen on the wall, ate popcorn, and cheered the Cavaliers on to victory! It was good for Fr. John to take a break from his rigorous schedule to relax and enjoy one of his favorite pastimes. Of course, being from a suburb of Cleveland, we enjoyed it also.

Day 10

This day was a treat for Marsha and me. For Mother's Day earlier in the year, her son had given her a bible that served us well in El Salvador. Each page was divided into two columns; one column was written in English and right next to it was a corresponding Spanish translation. With it, we were able to attend the bible study offered twice a month by one of the parishioners. Of course, our Spanish was minimal and, in the class, naturally everyone spoke Spanish, but we were able to understand most of the teaching with the help of the bi-lingual bible. We learned more during those times than bible passages. We learned that these people were welcoming, kind, and warm hearted. They were thrilled to share their faith and proud to have something of value to provide for us. We tried to speak Spanish and they tried to speak English as a gesture of solidarity. And of course, we all laughed together at our awkward but well-meaning attempts.

Day 11

It was a good thing we rested the previous day, because on this day we were on-the-go from morning until night. We began by attending Mass in Teotepeque wherein two little girls were going to receive their first communion. As always, it was a long but inspiring Mass.

When we returned to the rectory, Dalia, the housekeeper/cook, asked us to visit her sister's home. She was hosting a family gathering and wanted us to join in. Up until then, we had only met the families in the mountains for whom we were building house. This would give us a chance to experience what family life in the city of Teotepeque was really like. We walked from the rectory, down the hill and came upon Dalia's mother's house. We continued to walk farther down the hill following a wooded path that eventually brought us to two very modest houses in the woods. The first house was Dalia's sister's house, and about fifty feet even farther down the hill was Dalia's house.

There were around forty guests that moved freely between the three houses that had been built only steps away from each other. Dalia introduced us to everyone. We met her mother, her sister, her two brothers, a nephew, sisters-in-law, and nieces and nephews. We also recognized the two little girls who had made their First Communion at Mass earlier in the day. These two little girls were siblings and belonged to Dalia's younger sister. As introductions unfolded, the reason for the gathering became clear; we were there to celebrate one of the sacraments of initiation into the Catholic Church bestowed upon these two little girls—The Holy Eucharist (receiving communion of the Body and Blood of Christ). Everyone understood what that meant to this very large and faith-filled family; love, laughter, and joy filled everyone at the party. In the center of the festivities was a very large cake decorated to commemorate the meaning of this event.

We joined in and were treated just like family members. It was a special treat for us to meet one of Dalia's nephews who spoke English. We were thrilled to be able to talk to him at length. He was happy to interpret for us as we tried to communicate with our newfound family. We learned that he currently lived in Virginia and had been in the United States for over twenty years. Even though a generation had passed, he still felt as though his true home was El Salvador. His youth was spent in his native country during the El Salvadoran civil war. Since it was a bloody massacre of the poor, he admitted that, as a child, he was often afraid for his life. He recounted stories of how he would hide under his bed as he heard gun shots and screams just outside his house. He said he still senses fear rise up in him every time he comes to visit. His heart was torn; he loved his family in El Salvador and missed them every day, but he felt he had to leave to find a safer life for himself, his wife, and his children.

During this conversation, we were seated in Dalia's sister's house. But since the house was so small, many of the guests were standing outside near one of the adjacent houses. The home we were in seemed to be a typical home found in the city of Teotepeque. It was very old, supported by tree branches and some cinder block, and of course lamina for a roof.

As we made our way down to Dalia's house, we found it to be a tenuous task; we only had a rocky path to follow. Fortunately, her now deceased father had previously fashioned a handrail made of tree branches so the path up and down the hill would be safer for his wife and daughters. Upon arriving at Dalia's house, we were surprised to find a television and a refrigerator. Her house was one of the few houses in the small city that actually had electricity. The refrigerator and television had been given to her by an American friend. She was beyond thrilled to receive these gifts. And as you might imagine, her house became the gathering place for young and old alike. As the party progressed, the hostess began to set out the food. Of course, we couldn't eat any of the food that the family ate, but Dalia, in her infinite thoughtfulness, had specially prepared a few dishes that we could enjoy without the fear of intestinal problems. So, we ate, drank bottled water, took pictures and played games with everyone.

When it was time to return back to the rectory, the sun was beginning to set. Now, even though we had met some loving, welcoming people in the community, we still had to be aware that El Salvador was rated as one of the most dangerous countries in the world. Our experience and research taught us that gangs terrorized the big cities and we were not to visit them. Generally, the mountain areas were safer, but we had recently learned that some gang activity was finding its way into Teotepeque. As a result, it was unsafe for us to walk home alone. So, another one of Dalia's nephews offered to accompany us to ensure that we would arrive at the rectory safely.

We fell asleep quickly that night. It had been a long but satisfying day, and we were learning more about the people and country that we came to serve. Our hearts were growing fonder of our missionary work each day!

Day 12

I am adding this particular daily narrative so that you can "meet" Dalia, upfront and personal. I want you so see that poverty due to lack of opportunity does not necessarily translate into laziness or lack of initiative. Dalia's father brought his family up to Teotepeque to escape the carnage of the civil war in the cities in the 1970s. His family was one of the first groups of people who were actual refuges in their own country. They came to the mountains with nothing but the clothes on their backs, but this man carved out a home and a life for his wife and children. His hard work and dedication to raising his children was not lost on Dalia. She acquired his perseverance, his ability to educate himself through life experiences, and his nurturing nature. Here is an example of Dalia's ability to thrive.

On this particular day, Fr. John had to leave El Salvador and return to the United States for two weeks. He arose earlier than usual that morning in order to tie up some loose ends on his ongoing projects before he left. I had some questions for him regarding our duties while he was gone, but, being a man myself, I knew that my questions were not a priority at that moment, so I decided to rely on my own ingenuity while he was gone. By the time he settled down to thinking about the logistics of his trip, it was 9:15 a.m. He decided to see what time his flight was scheduled to leave. Since he couldn't find the paper that he wrote the information on, he decided just to look it up on the computer. He had the ability to rush a lot of things, but the computer was not one of them. So like all good managers, he called in for reinforcements, "Marsha, can you get the information I need for my flight?" After a few tense moments, she was able to find this flight information. Keep in mind the all the information was in Spanish and at that time, we were still not proficient in the language. We determined that the flight left at

12:30 p.m.; it was now 10:30 a.m. and the airport was about forty-five minutes away. We were able to print the boarding passes to help expedite the check in process at the airport.

It was at this moment that Dalia entered the game. Like a valuable sixth man coming off the bench, she hit the floor running. Suddenly Fr. John's clean laundry appeared out of nowhere—washed, dried, ironed and neatly folded. Next, she showed up with his vestments, on hangers and draped in plastic bags to keep them preserved and unwrinkled. Realizing that he wouldn't have time to eat at the airport, she then produced a freshly packed lunch and a cold drink that he could enjoy on his way to the airport.

Fr. John's mind then turned to a few last minute instructions for Marsha and me—explaining payroll duties, bill paying tasks and distributing keys to us. As time was ticking away, his energy level was ramping up; so many details, so little time. Not only that, several people were appearing at his door to snatch away the little time he had for their own questions and concerns. But Dalia was not to be foiled. In the spirit of the NBA, she started to set a screen for him to shield him from the other obstacles. Only through a video replay could we have seen that prior to setting the screen, she had cunningly opened up the passenger's side front door of the truck. That meant that Fr. John had a clear lane to the front seat. Judging from the fact that this move was so effective in helping him leave, I have to believe that it had been rehearsed over and over again. It was beautiful to behold. Fr. John entered the car without incident, and Rembe, his driver, jumped in the driver's seat and took it from there. It was very rare to find a driver as proficient as Rembe, and since no one pays attention to speed limits in El Salvador, Fr. John made it to the airport on time. Of course, Marsha and I were exhausted with his pace, but he had become a master at stretching time.

Day 13

By 8 a.m., Marsha and I were in the pickup truck with Rembe, Miguel (Fr. John's liturgical assistant), and Cesar (our interpreter) to visit a small village called Sihuapilapa Arriba high up on a mountainside. We were visiting a small church there to participate in a Celebration of Scripture. Miguel, whose position in the church was somewhat like that of an unofficial deacon, would preside over our gathering. Since he was not ordained, he could not consecrate the Eucharist, but he was very capable of interpreting scripture and conducting praise and worship services. In this region, the Mass is only celebrated once a month, at best, and sometimes even more rarely. So, these devout parishioners look forward to Miguel's visits to reconvene for the expressed purpose of nourishing the community of their faith.

The drive up the mountain seemed like a scene out of a Jurassic Park movie. Instead of facing dinosaurs, we faced dogs, chickens, pigs, wild horses, and an occasional steer. Our trail was muddy from the rains of the previous night and treacherous to navigate. Ninety-nine percent of the forty-five-minute drive was off the road on dirt paths laden with huge rocks. At times, the truck swerved back and forth as we tried to avoid the rocks. To those of us from the northern United States, it felt like we were sliding on icy roads during a January snowstorm. Adding to our stress, as I looked out my window, I could see that we were only a few feet away from the side of the mountain. One mistake by our driver could propel us over the edge causing us to land a couple of hundred feet down into the valley below. We all had confidence in Rembe's driving ability, but even that didn't stop us from uttering a few prayers under our breath.

Even though we were experiencing a degree of anxiety,

ascending to a mountain top, no matter where you are, is an inspiring experience. We tried to abandon our fears and focus on this new environment in which we found ourselves. As we gazed down on the earth below, we seemed to gain a new perspective. We were humbled as we realized that we were a very minuscule part of our great earth, of our expansive universe. We came to understand that we were assigned a very small moment in the eternal time line that began before we were born and would continue after our death. The proper response to this novel experience is one of gratitude; we could see so much beauty in God's creation and in His creatures. We became acutely aware of the need for unity among us all; a sense that we are companions on the journey, not competitors; brothers and sisters, not strangers. With the warmth of a sense of belonging, we were eager to reach our destination and meet our newfound family members.

It seemed like forever, but we finally reached the church and found the doors and windows wide open enabling a cool breeze to refresh us. Since we were early, we had time to take in the details of our surroundings. The church itself was small but had enough room to accommodate about fifty people. We walked around outside and found a large cornfield behind the church building. The cornfield was actually on the side of the mountain and dropped several hundred feet down toward the valley. At that time, we saw three people working in the field; one teenage boy, and two women. All three were bent over, each one swinging a large machete through the soil between the rows of corn. Stroke by stroke, they expertly used their knives tediously removing the stubborn weeds. We learned that it was necessary to clear out the weeds because, if left unattended, they would overtake the soil and choke the growth of the corn. At harvest time, their crops would be diminished, and much of their hard work would have been in vain. For a country with so little resources, it was paramount to salvage everything they could. The day grew hotter and hotter, and eventually all three of them picked up their water and tools and left the area. I could only imagine how time consuming and difficult it would be to clear the entire field. It was backbreaking work and surely it would take several weeks. However, their opportunities were few and their children were hungry, so they toiled on and on.

At that time, the parishioners were already seated and the celebration was about to begin. A few men, but mostly, women and children filled the church. Several people were standing outside. It was interesting to look at the congregation and wonder about the lives of these people. So many questions popped into our minds. *How could they be so desperately poor but still so joyful sing out praise and gratitude to their Lord? Could they even imagine the future? And if so, what did they see? Why did we see so few men at the church or in the field? Were the men working or have they abandoned their families? Would they have food for dinner that night? Clean drinking water? How could they be so generous to us and to their neighbors when they had next to nothing for themselves?*

The more time we spent with these people, the more we began to understand them. Eventually, the questions we had about them transformed into questions we had about ourselves. *We have so much, why aren't we more joyful? We are always looking into the future, why are we not content with the present day? After all, don't we ask our Lord to "give us this day our daily bread"? Why are missing the beauty of today just so we can pile up resources for the future? Do we share our abundant resources with our friends, family and God's poor? Are we aware of all there is to life beyond what our society and culture promises?* All of these questions were swirling around our minds as we began our journey down the mountain. There was so much to think about. We were warned that a mission trip would not only change the people we came to serve but it would change our own lives dramatically. While we could see this happening and were grateful at that time, we weren't yet fully aware of what that meant.

EIGHT

SOLIDARITY WITH THE POOR - WEEK 3

Day 16

Since the months of May to October are considered winter (*invierno* in Spanish) in El Salvador, we had been inundated with thunderstorms, torrential rains and deafening cracks of lightning during our sojourn here. The last few days had been particularly inclement so our Operation Rescue, Inc. workers were unable to traverse the muddy, slippery dirt paths up the mountain to get to their worksites. Therefore, our driver, Rembe, was available to us for whatever we needed. And since Dalia needed groceries, we decided to brave the weather and embark on a trip a little way down the mountain on a winding but paved road, to one of the bigger cities where we could shop at a store similar to the wholesale stores that we have in the US.

Because we had so much confidence in Rembe's skill as a driver, we were able to relax and enjoy the ride. The rains were intermittent, so even though we had times of low visibility and dark clouds, we also were given opportunities to see beautiful, vibrant rainbows and shafts of bright sunlight bursting through the trees brightening our pathway. Experiencing an electrical storm high up on a mountain and seeing rainbows arching over the valleys, I must admit, I was amazed at the power and beauty of nature. Once again Marsha and I were humbled and inspired. The beauty wasn't confined to nature; we saw it in the children playing in the puddles; in the women hanging their laundered clothes on tree branches trying to steal what little sunlight they could to dry their clothes; other young mother's walking along the road, toddlers in tow, balancing a basket of fruits and vegetables on their heads, looking for opportunities to sell their goods. To us, their lives seemed limited; to them, it was business as usual.

Having interacted with so many of these mountain-dwelling people, I found it hard to believe how kind and generous they were. So many without work; and those who do have an income share their resources with those who don't. I found one thing that was conspicuously obvious: **NO ONE** had a sense of entitlement; no one seemed resentful about their lot in life. Instead, they laughed, wore smiles on their faces, loved, and were committed to their faith. All of this is in spite of a lack of opportunity not only to envision their future, but also to feel secure in their daily lives. The mountain-dwelling people seemed to be able to enjoy each moment choosing not to stay focused on the pervasive fear of gang violence, political and government corruption, or the inevitable poverty that was the underpinning of their culture. I looked at them and wondered who the less fortunate were. *Was it the poor in the mountains of El Salvador, or those in the United States who found themselves better off financially, but lacked the spirit of gratitude and unity that we need to bind the human race? Could it be that God has called us here so that we might see how to reprioritize our values? Could it be that we are more the ones that need more help?* After all, in Matthew 6:31 – 34, Jesus says,

"Stop worrying over questions like, what are we to eat, or what are we to drink, or what are we to wear? Your heavenly Father knows all that you need. Seek first his kingship over you, his way of holiness, and all these things will be given to you besides."

We spend too much time in the United States being anxious, trying to get ahead, and working endless hours trying to accumulate more and more wealth. Should we not be more like the poor El Salvadoran mountain people, who worry less about food, shelter and drink, and what they wear, but rather seek God's kingdom and his righteousness? Ponder this scripture.

Day 21

Over the next few days, the rains persisted, and the mud seemed to spread everywhere. However, we came to this country for a purpose, rain or no rain. So, we headed to Mizata to visit each of the three families who were going to receive a new home. We needed to establish the order in which the houses were going to be built. All the families had immediate needs, so the undertaking of the day was going to be difficult. We connected with each family on an intimate level, but it would be challenging to prioritize which family would receive a house first.

We first had to travel up the mountain in precarious conditions. Luckily, for this trip, the road was paved, but muddy, slippery, and littered with rocks and boulders that slid down the mountainside directly in our path. Add to these conditions an array of oblivious indigenous animals who considered the road to be specifically for their own use. Driving through areas where rain swollen streams crossed over the road posed a threat, we were undaunted in our quest and our enthusiasm did not wane. So Marsha and I packed our rain gear, picked up the lunch that Dalia packed for us, and piled into the pickup truck. Once again, Rembe was our driver, Miguel was our guide, and Cesar was our interpreter. We were a good team for the job; all of us contributed something valuable for this humanitarian effort.

When we arrived at Mizata, we were met by the council member of this community who would accompany the five of us to the dwellings of each of the three families we were to meet. Miguel had already scheduled an interview with each family in advance so that Marsha and I could meet as many members of the families as possible. We needed to know how many adults and how many children would be residing in the house we were to build. This information was important for us to prioritize the order in which the houses would be built.

In addition to the practical value of these interviews, interacting with the people of all ages was paramount for us to keep alive the *why* of our mission to help God's poor. After all, the whole concept of Christianity is that God interacted with us in the person of Jesus to demonstrate His love for us in a tangible way. We wanted to convey that same type of love to these isolated, forgotten people. Consequently, each time I met the adult members of the families to receive a house, I extended my hand and said, "I have been looking forward to meeting you. We have traveled from our home in North America, over three thousand miles just to greet the family that God has chosen to receive a home. You are very important to Him and to us. It is our pleasure to serve you!" Of course, this was all conveyed through our interpreter Cesar. Each time I said these words, tears of gratitude welled up in their eyes. They were unaccustomed to any reference to their personal value. Never had they imagined that anyone cared about them and their plight so much. To them, America was the "land of milk and honey," a place so far away and out of their reach that they could only fantasize about it. Now, they had a friend, an advocate, from America, who cared enough about them to change their circumstances, their current lives, and their future. *How could this be?* They could only respond "Gloria a Dios!" (Thanks be to God!)

After an hour-long truck ride, and a thirty-minute trek on foot up the mountain over rocks and through a few ankle-deep creeks, we made it to our first destination. We were greeted by a young mother, Maria Blanco. The expression on her face conveyed her unspoken joy and anticipation of our visit. As usual, wherever we went children appeared and this was no exception. Never having seen Americans before they were a bit shy, but their inquisitiveness prevailed. We always brought a bag of lollipops with us on these excursions. We showed them to their mother and pointed to the children. After she nodded, I offered them to the children. At this gesture, their shyness dissipated, and we immediately became newfound friends.

With the help of our interpreter, Maria began telling us about her family. Maria was thirty-two and had given her husband, José, four children; the three boys were Delmi, age 3; Candelasiur, age 6; and Daniel, age twelve. The oldest was a sixteen-year-old daughter named Maria Estella. José, her husband, was thirty-seven and worked in a restaurant as a cook. Because they had no means of transportation and lived so far up in the mountains, getting to work was a lengthy and arduous endeavor. For that reason, he would stay at the restaurant for two weeks at a time before he returned to his family for a one week stay. It was a difficult schedule for very little compensation, but they were grateful for the opportunity to work at all.

Why would a family choose to live so far up in the mountains if the head of the household worked so far away in a city down the mountain? One important reason was that they owned the property that they lived on, which ensured them, and us, that there would be no chance of a landlord evicting them after the property was improved with a stable house. The other reason, perhaps the most important of all, was the rampant and deadly gang violence in the El Salvadoran cities. In order to increase the number of young boys committed to allegiance to their gang, they routinely kidnapped young boys and force them to join their gang. If they refused, they were threatened with the loss of their lives or the loss of the lives of their siblings. These young boys were usually either found dead, or never heard of again. It was a crushingly painful fear that all the families lived with daily. Even though living in the mountains far away from the cities had its difficulties, it also provided some emotional security for the families.

Having completed our initial greeting, we asked Maria if she would mind showing us around and asked if we could take a few pictures of her dwelling. She was eager to comply. The floor was nothing but dirt, the walls were made of tree branches and dried, cracked mud, and the roof was made of worn tin weakened by holes and rust. Because our visit was in the rainy season, the water from the torrential rains poured into the house through the holes in the roof and rendered the floor damp, muddy and slippery. The family had given up trying to wear shoes, which quickly ended up laden with layers of mud, making it difficult to even walk around. To avoid that problem, the entire family walked around with their bare feet. They couldn't avoid the mud, but they learned to be careful of the deep puddles, red ants, scorpions, and the rats that often invaded their abode.

There was no electricity in the house, no windows, and obviously no ventilation. Consequently, when we went inside, we were overcome with a musty odor that hung in the air. The only small bit of light in the house (it was midday) came through the holes in the rusty roof. It was insufficient to really see anything, so I immediately switched on a small battery-operated lamp I carried with me. My heart stopped at what I saw. From this perspective, it was clear that the mud that formed the walls was infested with insects that were similar to chiggers. They not only bore holes in the walls, letting in moisture, but also posed a serious health threat to adults and children alike. There were a couple of make-shift beds for the children, and hammocks that served as beds for the adults. Everything was filthy, moldy, and decrepit. As I looked around and saw the condition that family lived in, I was so grateful that this family was chosen to receive a house from Operation Rescue, Inc. I could not imagine spending a night there, let alone to call this my home. These were unfamiliar surroundings to us, and we made no judgements, as we knew this family was doing the very best they could considering the circumstances they faced. This family has come to accept living this way; and in some unfathomable sense felt somewhat proud to show us around. They were proud of their children, proud that they had been able to live as a connected family, and proud that somehow, they were able to survive these conditions. So, perhaps proud was the wrong word; I think grateful would have been a better choice.

After some hugs and more lollipops, we were off to our next destination. The second family we were to visit was only about a quarter of a mile up the mountain. There we were met by Soyla Noemi Diaz. Soyla was a thirty-five-year-old mother of two children; Sarsa, a five-year-old daughter and José, a nine-year-old son. Soyla's husband, Santos, was not home at that time. He worked in the fields belonging to a farmer. He was not compensated in money, but rather in food to feed his family. That is the only way they could survive; but they still had no money for medical care, personal care items, clothes, etc. They had no electricity, but they did have a rather unique system of capturing rainwater that was stored in two large, metal drums. They were happy to have clean water for drinking and cooking, but beyond that, their circumstances were almost identical to the previous family.

As I looked at this young mother of two, I felt the emptiness in her; her eyes conveyed a look of desperation, of giving up on life. She answered all of our questions and said that she was glad that her family had been chosen for a new house. But her body told another story; something was missing, as though all the life had been drained from her body, leaving her only a shell of a person. The word *zombie* came to my mind. Nothing I offered her changed the expression on her face. When I told her that God had chosen her family and that we were grateful to meet her, she still remained emotionless. When we left her, I did not take with me the usual feeling that Operation Rescue, Inc. was improving her life.

Instead, I had to wrestle with several questions. *Would the gift of this "casita" (small house) make a difference in her life? Would it lift her spirits? Would it give her hope for the future? For the future of her children? Were there even any desires in her anymore?* I pondered these questions for a length of time and before I received an answer. It was a *Yes* based on faith alone. I found my answer when I remembered a section of a prayer written by Monsignor Oscar Romero. He wrote, *"As missionaries, we are working toward a goal that we may never see accomplished in our lifetime. We are not to be discouraged or in despair. We are to remain vigilant and dedicated to our goal and trust that the completion of our work is in the hands of God, according to his timeline."*

I carried this wisdom with me as we made our way to our final destination of the day. This one was even more isolated, if that is even possible. Driving through areas where rain swollen streams overtook the road and posed a serious threat to our progress, we were undaunted, and our enthusiasm did not wane. Soon the road became a primitive path and we had to disembark from our vehicle and rely on our ability to hike up the path. This, of course, included more steams, slippery rocks and wet shoes.

As we approached the family, we saw a host of people anticipating our visit. Our first encounter was with Papá, otherwise known as Leopoldo Hernandez, the seventy-five-year-old owner of this parcel of land. As he sat shirtless in his hammock, it was as though he, and only he, would stand guard over their property ready to ward off threats from inhospitable strangers. But when he saw us approaching, he quickly rose to his feet, a smile broke out lighting up his entire face. He began speaking Spanish a mile a minute. How I wish I could have understood his emotional words! As it turned out, he wasn't a guard as much as he was the head of the family who took his responsibility to welcome guests very seriously. We followed him

71

toward the dwelling and soon met Mamá, his wife, sitting in her own hammock. Her name was Victoria Diaz Hernandez, age seventy-two, a proud woman of few words who was equally eager to greet us. The family heard our greetings and all came out to meet us. Sonia Marlene Hernandez was their thirty-five-year-old daughter. She was noticeably taller than most of the people we had met; she stood at least six-feet tall and towered over everyone, including her parents. There was something about her demeanor that was gentle but yet commanded respect. She introduced herself and quickly asked us to be seated while she remained standing. At this point, all the children were waiting to be introduced. First, we met Jefferson, her eight-year-old son. He was accompanied by his three-year-old sister, Fatima de Cusmer. They were very well behaved, as they surely did not want to be excluded from this conversation. Standing in the doorway, we also noticed two more of Sonia's children; Pedro her eleven-year-old son, and Soledad her fourteen-year-old daughter. There was also another sixteen-year-old boy who stayed inside, visible only by his silhouette, almost completely hidden by the dark interior of the house. He was a boy that Sonia volunteered to raise. He quickly disappeared back into the recesses of the house. We never learned any more of his history.

We understood from our interpreters that Papá owned the property we were visiting. Sonia and the children under her care were living there so that she could take care of her parents. She was a single mother and life had forced her to take charge of her situation, and take charge she did! She earned an income by selling beef and fish in order to sustain this large family. She said, "God provides but it has taken a lot of prayers and help along the way." Despite the weight of so much responsibility, Sonia was not downtrodden at all, rather she was full of life, strength, and determination. Her love for her mother and father, and the needs of her children were what gave her reason to get up every morning. She showed us around the house and we found the same issues as we found in previous houses—insect-infested mud walls, dirt floors, holes in the roof, and make-shift beds. Utensils and clothes were in disarray mostly because there were no cupboards, closets, or storage spaces. Nonetheless, Sonia seemed proud to show us her dwelling. Her demeanor was in stark contrast to that of Sonia from the house we visited prior to this one.

However, when we began to leave, Sonia's tough exterior began to crumble. It started at the moment that I told her that God had chosen her to receive a house from Operation Rescue, Inc. I explained that He had seen how hard she was working to keep the family together; and He wanted to bless her efforts. I could see the weight of the responsibility on her shoulders lighten. Tears welled up in her eyes, and gratitude covered her weathered face. She reached out for my shoulder and I felt the sincerity of her touch—the compassion of a dedicated mother and daughter, and the relief of a strong but sensitive woman.

Day 22

Before I recount what happened on this day, I must give you a little background so you can fully appreciate this story. There was a homeless, blind man that walked the streets of Teotepeque. We had seen him many times, wandering the streets, sitting on porches during the rains, and spending time in the courtyard of the church we were serving. He loved to come to the rectory; he knocked on the door often around noon. He knew that Dalia would always prepare a lunch for him. She was always thoughtful and generous with him. She was considerate of the fact that he didn't have any teeth so she would prepare freshly cooked meals for him always aware of what he could and could not eat.

On this particular day, Fr. John was still visiting the United States, and we had told Dalia that she could take a few days off to care for her family. We would be able to eat leftovers or cook something for ourselves. We were doing fine on our own until this particular day. We had gotten up and Marsha made breakfast. The morning went fast as we cleaned up the kitchen and our living space. I spent some time writing and Marsha spent some time reading when all of a sudden, our peaceful day was interrupted with a knock on the door. We were a little startled because everyone in the community knew that Fr. John and Dalia were gone. We had been cautioned about the dangers of El Salvador so we were unsure whether we should open the door or not. When I went to the door and looked out the window, I didn't see anyone, so I opened the door. And then I saw the poor, homeless man sitting on the floor of the porch. I had no idea what to do, so I immediately called for Marsha to come to the door. Her Spanish had been improving so she was able to talk to the man and discovered that he was there to collect his lunch. He knew that Fr. John did not allow him to enter the rectory, so he was willing to wait on the porch until we brought some food. There were a few things in the refrigerator, but nothing he could eat since he had no teeth. Marsha would have made him scrambled eggs, but we were out of eggs. Then she came up with the idea to make him a peanut butter and jelly sandwich. We paired that with some applesauce and orange juice. Not your typical gourmet lunch but a meal nonetheless.

We brought it out to him to eat on the porch while we went back inside. After about an hour, we went back out to the porch; he had eaten and gone on his way, politely leaving the bowl, spoon, and glass that we gave him to use. We were pretty proud that we figured out what to do on our own, and happy that we abided by the following scripture passage:

"Whatsoever you do to the least of my brothers, that you do unto me."

Matt. 25:40

So, the next day, we waited for him to come again, but he did not come. So, day after day, we waited, but for days we did not see him again. We began to worry if he was still alive. Well, after Dalia returned to the rectory, he began to come for lunch again. We told her our story of providing lunch for him and asked why he hadn't come for so long. She smiled and kindly informed us that he hates peanut butter and didn't want to have to eat it ever again.

NINE

SOLIDARITY WITH THE POOR – WEEK 4

Day 25

This week promised to be a busy one so we woke up early and began planning the logistics that we hoped would allow for a stress-free schedule. Fr. John had been out of town for a few days so we wanted to make sure that when he returned, he would find that Marsha, Dalia and I had been able to work independently during his absence. He arrived on time and without incident, so we were off to a good start.

Around noon, we all headed to the Mission House to prepare lunch for or a group of about twenty members of a church from Cleveland, Ohio, who were there to spend a week studying the culture of the area. Dalia had previously purchased enough food and beverages for the group for the entire week. The store she shopped at to get the best prices was about an hour away. It was difficult to make the trip but worth the trouble. The luncheon that day went well; thanks to Dalia's attention to detail.

After lunch, we accompanied Fr. John and Miguel as they

presided over a funeral; the second in as many days. Miguel had the experience to conduct a funeral and prayer service even if Fr. John was not available. This funeral followed the same format as the one I previously detailed for Erika. The homily was inspiring, and the music was comforting. We had an uneventful ride back to the rectory and we were beginning to think that all of our organizational efforts were paying off. That is until early the next morning . . .

Day 26

Early in the morning, Fr. John received a phone call from Dalia. She was unusually upset. She explained that when she arrived at the Mission House at 6 a.m., she found that the refrigerator stopped working during that night. This was the same refrigerator that contained a week's worth of food and drinks for our twenty guests from Cleveland. It was no longer cold enough to keep the perishable food from spoiling in the sweltering heat of Teotepeque. Fr. John always said, "This is El Salvador; nothing works here!" With his experience he was used to quickly formulating alternative plans. He gathered Marsha, Rembe, and I, and instructed us to go to the city of La Libertad and purchase a new refrigerator. Keep in mind that La Libertad was labeled one of the most dangerous cities in the world by the US government; one that they advised travelers not to visit because of its propensity to gang violence. However, Rembe was a fearless bodyguard. We trusted his judgement, and had faith in his ability to keep us safe. Whenever he drove us anywhere, he would not let Marsha out of his sight; he always stayed within six feet of her while she visited schools, churches, or worksites. I was grateful for that because on a few occasions, Marsha got caught up in the joy of meeting the indigenous people and did not focus on the fact that she was in a dangerous country.

Before we were able to leave on our trip, we had one very important task to complete; we had to confer with Dalia. She was a great employee of Fr. John's and usually complied with his bidding whenever she could. But he was also a good employer and gave her full authority on certain topics. Deciding on what kind of refrigerator to purchase was one of those topics. But since I didn't speak Spanish and she didn't speak English, I had to figure out a way to understand exactly what kind of refrigerator Dalia wanted. At that point in time, we did have access to the internet and I had my computer, so I went online and found websites for stores in La Libertad. Although Dalia had little worldly experience, she was very confident about what qualities she insisted on in a refrigerator. She immediately pointed out that the size needed to be 20 cubic feet, and it had to have a top freezer with no ice maker. I wondered why but dared not ask. Fr. John's only requirement was that we did not want to spend more than $800.00. In addition to that, he preferred a Frigidaire.

So, we piled into the truck hopeful but quite uncertain whether or not we could find the specified refrigerator, for the cost we needed, that was available to bring back that same day in Rembe's truck. The first store we went to did not carry Frigidaire. The second one had several, but they were too small. The third store had a Frigidaire with a top freezer and no ice maker. But the cost was $1,000. As we approached the fourth store, I knew that we were running out of options, but for some reason, I said to Marsha, "This is it! This is the store where we are going to find our refrigerator!"

As we entered the store, we saw that the appliance department was along the back wall. A few more steps and Marsha spotted a large, top-freezer refrigerator. And it happened to be a Frigidaire! However, we still had two problems, it had an automatic ice maker and the cost was $1,000. Still undaunted, I asked the saleswoman in my broken Spanish, if she had any without ice makers. She thought for a moment, and explained in her broken English, "Let me see. I may have one last one on the showroom floor." She walked us over to the corner and there it was, our refrigerator. But only one more question: How much did it cost? You won't believe this . . . $799! The only thing standing between us and the perfect purchase price was the tax. At this point, I said, "Write it up!" She said it was the only one remaining, but we could have it if we could wait until it could be moved to the pick-up area. Of course, we were willing to wait. After taking my name, she announced that I owed a total amount of $799. I thought to myself, no tax? This was going so well, I decided not to complicate the sale and forget about the tax. I handed her $800 and held my breath. A few minutes later, she handed me a receipt and a good old American dollar! They loaded the refrigerator onto the truck, and we started to leave the parking lot. At that moment, Rembe asked me if I had any more money, since we needed to pay a fee for parking. All I had was the dollar I received for change, so I gave it to him, and he gave it to the gatekeeper. The gate opened and we were on our way back to the mission house. The total amount Fr. John had given us was $800. We had gotten the perfect refrigerator, including the parking toll, for $800! *Divine intervention?* Absolutely!

Once again, we learned that if God wanted it done, it would be done. We just felt privileged to witness the presence of God in our lives.

Day 27

As much as we looked forward to this day, it turned out to be one of the most physically challenging experiences we had had to date. We had seen pictures, heard stories, and met the recipient families, but had never been to a worksite in progress. So, this day we would get to see full scope of grueling labor it took to make our dream come true. We ventured out at seven in the morning. Marsha and I were seated in the cab of the truck with Rembe, while three of our workers, along with Miguel and Chepe sat in the bed of the truck. Chepe accompanied us on our treks only periodically. Because he was not only the local administrator of the project, but also Miguel's son, he had a vested interest in the progress of workers. Our plan was to travel to a worksite and watch the builders physically build one of the Operation Rescue, Inc. houses. Of course, all of the visits up the mountains were difficult, but on this trip, we encountered so many deep potholes on the roads that we were bounced around mercilessly. The workers in the back bed of the truck were hanging on to the railings and had to make sure their tools were not damaged or worse yet, thrown off the truck.

We thought the ride in the truck was perilous, but then we had to hike one-half mile up the mountain. This path was about three feet wide, slippery, and littered with huge boulders. Marsha and I only had to carry food, water, bug spray, our camera and some emergency first aid items. The workers had to carry not only the large and extremely heavy tool chest, but also a variety of addition building supplies. One of the workers was a man, I would say in his late thirties, of short stature but with strong arms. He carried a gas-powered generator on his back all the way to the worksite. I was thinking that if I put him up against the line backers of any of our NFL teams, he would surely win their respect!

Upon arrival of the worksite, we met the man for whom the house was being built. He was so eager to greet us that the minute we got within his line of vision, you could just see the joy emanating from his whole body. He smiled from ear to ear, and his eyes filled with tears of gratitude; and we could almost hear his heart beating with anticipation. This expression of happiness told us all we needed to know about what this house would mean to him and his family. As we have said before, once we arrived, it didn't take long for the children to show up, and this was no exception. The first to arrive this day was a six your old little girl who was carrying her ten-month-old little brother. We exchanged greetings in Spanish; the language barrier seemed to dissipate when we were interacting with children. We knew we were in for a long day, so we began looking for a place to sit down and actually see the hard, physical labor it took to make our dream become a reality. We found some rocks on the side of the mountain just above the worksite that we could use. At this point, some of the older children showed up, two more girls and two more boys all between the ages of nine and fifteen. One of the older girls brought a bench for us to sit on. Since we were on a slanted surface that was unstable due to all the mud, I had to secure the legs with some smaller rocks. Once I did that, we had a fairly comfortable place to site with a perfect view of the activities below us.

It was quite an experience watching our builders. By this time, they had been working together for a length of time. They exchanged few words, but their actions appeared to be carefully choreographed; they wasted no time or energy on this extremely hot and humid day. The foundation and floor had been completed previously, so on this day, there were able to construct the walls. By the afternoon, they ready for some of the specialized workers to put on the finishing touches for the house.

Some worked on framing in the window space; some began mixing fresh concrete for the support beams needed to secure the roof. Steel rods had to be welded to the beams, and cement filled every gap around those beams. Once in place, it would then be time to attach the one-inch-thick lamina to the beams. This lamina was strong enough that it would remain viable and hole-free for eighteen to twenty years before needing to be replaced. While the roof was being secured, the metal window, shutters, and door were being painted. Another worker was applying a layer of cement over the foundation blocks covering up to about twenty inches of the walls. This would help to serve as a protective barrier to prevent ground-level water from being absorbed into the walls and subsequently into the house. The inside beams were also getting a protective layer of cement in an effort to close all the holes, in addition to a coat of paint to help with waterproofing. It took six workers a total of five hours to attach the door, the window space shutters, support beams and the roof to this new house. The finishing touches were completed.

At this point, we were ready to leave and make our way down the mountain path to the road where our pick-up truck was parked. We said our final good-byes to the owner and his wife. They were speechless and overwhelmed. I simply placed my hands on my heart and pointed to the sky. The Lord had given them this house, make no mistake about that. The donating family, the workers, and the administrators of Operation Rescue, Inc. had simply said *yes* to God's invitation to take care of His poor.

Getting the tool chest down the mountain was indeed a chore. However this time, neighbors of the family that received the house were willing to help. Equally helpful were the older children, who carried shovels, picks, buckets, and large water containers for us. We also had a second crew working in the adjacent area on another house, so when we picked them up, they added all of their equipment with ours filling the back of the truck. Transportation was so scarce that we had to "double-up" whenever we could. The truck was beyond full with all the tools and workers in the back bed. I was thinking that this would certainly be some kind of safety violation in the United States, but in El Salvador, you simply did what you had to do to get the job done. At that point, it was Rembe's job to get us back down the mountain and on to the highway. We made it safe and sound, but from there we had to travel one-half hour to Mizata where we were scheduled to build three more houses.

When we arrived at our destination, waiting for us on the side of the road was the young mother that we had spoken to just a few days earlier. Her big smile welcomed us, but it was her fifty-four-year-old father who was the highlight of our visit. I had never seen anyone so overtly excited to see someone. We got out of the truck and he came running up to me asking me if I was from the United States of America. I pointed to the name of Operation Rescue, Inc. on my shirt and said, "Yes I am!" He immediately grabbed me and gave me an embrace. Just then he spotted Marsha getting out of the truck and took off running to greet her in a similar manner. He then began helping our workers carry the huge tool chest up the mountain. The tool chest had to weigh at least 300 pounds and proved to be too much to handle for a man of his age. So, he enlisted his son-in-law to help him. As he tried to lift the box, every blood vessel in his neck popped out. But his will to help won out over his physical strength as they made their way up the mountain side. As I watched, I just prayed that neither of them would collapse under the weight of their burden.

As we approached the worksite, we caught sight of the faces of the receiving family. It was truly something to behold. Every family member, young and old shared the excitement of a new future, a secure home, and a safe lifestyle. Once again, I understood, we all understood the goodness of our God. However, by this time of day, sunlight was waning allowing only an hour or so for the workers to complete the work they had hoped to accomplish before heading to their respective homes. They made the most of the time they had and wasted not one minute. By the time the sun set, they were exhausted but relieved to have met their daily goal. It had been forty-five days since they last saw their families and they were looking forward to reuniting with their wives and children. Again, we loaded up the truck and headed home to Teotepeque. The workers would only take a few days off, and then travel back to Mizata to complete the last three houses there.

Prior to Operation Rescue, Inc. these same men were unemployed and unable to find any steady work. However, with Operation Rescue, Inc., they had not only a reliable income but also a trade, skills and experience that no one could ever take away from them. One of our objectives was *"offering employment opportunities that will lead to an independent and sustainable life-style."* What we were able to give these men was not only employment and a paycheck, but also pride in the ability to provide for their families. You could see the self-esteem rising their eyes, their work ethic, and their self-confidence. They were also modeling behavior that could only have a positive influence on their children. Seeds were being planted. Who knows where, when, or how they would grow and produce positive changes in these people and their culture.

Day 30

We have recounted a general idea as to what it takes to select a recipient family and what it takes to build a house. *But what does it take to make it a home?* Fr. John, whether intentionally or not, created a custom whereby this small, barren, block building could become a warm and welcoming home. We respectfully referred to this process as the "Blessing of the Home." It was a simple gesture on our part, but a very significant one for the new homeowners. After the family had moved into the house that Operation Rescue, Inc. built, Fr. John, and/or Miguel, and Marsha and I if we were available, went together to the location of the house. Occasionally we were accompanied by other missionaries from churches in the US who were visiting Teotepeque at that time. We brought a few gifts for the family; sacks of uncooked rice and beans, a small hand painted cross, a dedication plaque, and Holy Water. One other unique and totally unexpected gift was what looked like a light switch, however, was in fact used to produce light inside the dark house. It was battery operated and magnetic so that it could be attached to the metal door or the house or the metal window shutters.

On this particular day, we planned to visit two houses and offer the Blessing of the Home at each house. The first one, as you might imagine by now, was far up the mountain. As usual, we rode together in the truck as far as it could go, and then proceeded on foot. When we got out of the truck, we seemed to be on a high ridge of a mountain. We looked into the valley before us and saw the tiny house nestled in a cornfield about two hundred and fifty feet below us. It was a beautiful scene as we stood there and contemplated how we were going to get down to the house. Its beauty faded a little as we marched down the mountain with our supplies, through the cornfield, in the high altitude and blistering heat. We were then informed that we must be very cautious while walking through the corn fields since it was a haven for poisonous snakes. At that point there was nothing we could to do but keep walking, looking down and reminding ourselves why we had put ourselves in this situation.

When we safely arrived at the first house, no one was home. We were understandably disappointed, but we left our gifts at the door, recited our blessing prayer, and hung the cross on the outside of the house. The last thing we did before departing was to attach the dedication sign to the house. It was a sign written in both English and Spanish. It said that the house was built by Operation Rescue, Inc. and listed the name or names of the donors who provided the funds to build the house. In some cases, the house was donated in honor of a deceased relative and if so the name of the relative was also included. These plaques were very important to the recipients of the house. They felt edified in some sense because they had the name of an advocate in the United States. Part of what we wanted to do for them was to honor their value and underscore the significance of their lives; the plaque highlighted their dignity.

TEN

SOLIDARITY WITH THE POOR - WEEKS FIVE AND SIX

Day 38

This was a day that Marsha had looked forward to for quite a while. A bible study was beginning, and we sat in attendance at 8 a.m. in a classroom of the second floor of the Academy that was on the school grounds. We were joined by about forty-two young adults who were all gathered to learn more about scripture. Each one was excited to have the opportunity to interact, their bible and notebook in hand. As mentioned before, one of Marsha's sons gave her a bilingual bible for Mother's Day; each page was divided into two columns, one in English and the other in Spanish. Needless to say, she was thrilled because this book contained the two things she thoroughly enjoyed, scripture and the chance to learn a new language.

All of the attendees were seriously engaged in the presentation. I was impressed with the questions they asked and the comments they offered, but my mind was wandering as I began to ask myself, *Why were these people so interested in learning about scripture?* They seemed to be pondering not only what they were learning, but also how to apply these principles to their everyday life. *Could it be that their poverty has taught them that they could not depend on themselves, but simply that they had to depend on the providence of their Lord? Has hoping in mere mortals disappointed them so many times, that they have redirected their hope to Jesus Christ; believing that all things are possible with Him?*

In our Western culture, many of us practice our faith through our words, not really through the actions of our everyday lives. Many of us have been taught, "If it's to be, it's up to me." We have come to believe that we are in control of our own destiny. We revere and strive for independence, rather than dependence on God. *Can we draw the conclusion that the more affluent the society, the more difficult it is to embrace the humility and servitude of Jesus Christ? As we work to gain success, do we leave Jesus on the side lines of our daily lives to offer only an occasional glance or a small gesture of thanks? Even worse, has Jesus become a silent observer in our lives waiting for an invitation to become acknowledged or recognized?*

Day 41

The Mission Team from St. Rita's Church in Solon, Ohio arrived the day before and on this day we were busy getting them settled in at the mission house and comfortable with their new surroundings. This generous parish had supported Operation Rescue, Inc. from its inception. Over the previous three years, they had donated over $35,000 that funded seventeen houses. We had a great desire to show these faithful parishioners the fruits of their donations. It is not often that those who give to charities ever get this kind of chance, and we were proud to be able to provide it. We arranged for transportation to take them to visit a few of the houses they provided. They were thrilled to meet the families that received their houses and the families were overwhelmed to meet their benefactors from America. The same scenario played out at each location; joyful tears, hugs, and smiles broke out as soon as we approached each house.

We regretted that we were not able to show them all the houses they funded but Marsha was able to put together a power point presentation to show the group later that evening. Her original intent was to document how and where all of their money had been applied. It started out like a business meeting with a balance sheet, but it ended much differently. Let me explain.

The group that gathered that evening consisted of adults and teenagers from St. Rita's Church, two teachers from the school, a few students, and members of another Missionary Team that was visiting at that time. We had eaten dinner together and stayed on to discuss the school and Operation Rescue, Inc. As the meeting began, the segment about the school was first on the agenda; it was presented by one of the Spanish speaking missionaries. After that, Marsha presented the facts and figures pursuant to our charity. She then began to speak from her heart and explained the *Why* behind our commitment. She shared how she was called to serve the poor at a very young age; and that she was so pleased to learn that I shared that same calling. She asked everyone in attendance to search their hearts and open their minds to hear the calling that our Lord had for each one of them. Then, she asked the teenagers, "You are here in this poverty-stricken country, meeting these families, playing with these children, attending Mass with young and old alike. Why are you here? You don't speak their language, yet you communicate with them on a very intimate level. How could that be? You will be forever changed by this experience. Who will you be when you return home? What is our Lord's invitation to you now?" She then played a song and asked everyone to sit in silence for a few minutes and ponder the words of the song. As the music came to a close, she read a prayer written by then Arch Bishop Oscar Romero from El Salvador. He was canonized on October 14, 2018, and is currently a saint.

It helps, now and then, to step back
and take a long view.
The kingdom is not only beyond our efforts,
it is even beyond our vision.
We accomplish in our lifetime only a tiny fraction
of the magnificent enterprise that is God's work.

*Nothing we do is complete, which is a way of saying
that the kingdom always lies beyond us.
No statement says all that could be said.
No prayer fully expresses our faith.
No confession brings perfection.
No pastoral visit brings wholeness.
No program accomplishes the church's mission.
No set of goals and objectives includes everything.*

*That is what we are about.
We plant the seeds that one day will grow.
We water seeds already planted,
knowing that they hold future promise.
We lay foundations that will need
further development.
We provide yeast that produces
far beyond our capabilities.
We cannot do everything and there is
a sense of liberation in realizing that.*

*This enables us to do something,
and to do it very well.
It may be incomplete, but it is a beginning,
a step along the way,
an opportunity for the Lord's grace to enter
and do the rest.*

*We may never see the end results,
but that is the difference
between the master builder and the worker.
We are workers, not master builders,
ministers, not messiahs.
We are prophets of a future not our own.*

Amen

————

The room was quiet for a few seconds after the end of the prayer, but then, all of a sudden, the audience erupted into applause. The teenagers in the room bounced up to Marsha, encircled her and one by one hugged her. They were giddy with enthusiasm for the awakening they experienced and were excited to discover more about their newfound calling. She was humbled by the acceptance of her message and filled with gratitude at the realization that they heard God's voice in her words.

By the end of the day, we were physically and emotionally exhausted. We slept well that night, with smiles on our faces.

Day 44

Dawn came too quickly on the next morning. It was the day before Fr. John hosted his monthly meeting with the canton leaders. The last time we met, the leaders made us aware that there were several families who needed help but did not qualify to be recipients of totally new houses. However, the roofs on their houses were also riddled with holes that allowed the torrential rains of the region to seep in and permeate all their belongings, meager as they were, with damaging moisture. This, in turn, led to mud, mold, and insect infestations throughout their living quarters. It was disheartening to imagine toddles running around and babies crawling on the floors of their homes in these conditions.

Since Operation Rescue, Inc. was created to raise the living conditions to basic humanitarian standards of these communities, we were able to expand the scope of our work to include replacing the roofs of existing houses. We first discussed this idea with the canton leaders at the previous monthly meeting, so this month we wanted to be fully prepared to provide them with what they asked for as soon as possible. It was important to be diligent and dedicated to this project because this segment of the population had been promised help so many times before; and was disappointed time and time again when the help never materialized. If we had let this plea for help slip through the cracks, it would serve to reinforce their deep-seated fear that no one really cared about them, and that they were not worthy of our time, attention, and resources. With that being said, it was time for us to crunch the numbers of how many families we could help, how many pieces of lamina we could afford to purchase, and how many we could give to each family. We also had to work out the logistics of how to get the lamina up the mountain to the selected families.

So, Fr. John, Marsha, and I put our heads together and started calculating. Each sheet of lamina would cost $6.60. We decided that we needed about nine hundred sheets resulting in a total cost of $5,940. This amount was within our $6,000 budget for this project, so we were making progress. The funds in our budget included a $5,000 donation from a kind, generous woman from St. Rita's Church, who specifically asked that this amount be spent on lamina. The remaining $1,000 came from corporate donations to be used in any way necessary to meet our mission statement goals.

Fr. John informed us that we would be serving twenty-three cantons. At $6.60 a sheet, and forty sheets of lamina per canton, the number of sheets we would need to purchase would be a total of nine hundred twenty sheets. That brought our total cost up to $6,072, slightly above our budget. Marsha and I pitched in the extra $72 needed to correct our balance sheet. Marsha was our treasurer; she was a good fit for the role because, while flexible on most things, accounting was not one of them. Every expenditure had to be necessary, well documented, and in line with our objectives. These calculations allowed us to give forty sheets of lamina to each of the cantons. Since five sheets of lamina were required for each roof, we could serve eight families in each canton. A total of one hundred eighty-four families would get a new roof. With these calculations completed, our next task was to create an orderly distribution process. Marsha designed, typed up, and printed out one hundred eighty-four numbered tickets, one for each bundle of five sheets of lamina. The tickets were printed with three different colors of ink on special paper purchased in La Libertad. As Marsha was printing sheets of tickets, I cut them into individual tickets and embossed them with an imprint of Fr. John's official seal. This was done to prevent anyone from trying to fabricate an unauthorized ticket in an attempt to acquire more lamina than they were entitled to receive. To easily track the ticket distribution, the canton name was printed on each numbered ticket. Once each leader was given their eight tickets, they could distribute to the families they chose to receive a lamina bundle. Fr. John had the idea to charge each family $1.00 for each sheet of lamina. This was done in order for them to understand that this was not merely a hand-out but rather a hand-up. They money collected was put into the general fund and used to help with future humanitarian projects. What started out to be simply a good idea, turned out to be a huge logistic time-consuming process. By the time we were finished with these preparations, it was 3 a,m.

Day 45

Fr. John woke up early to attend to his daily tasks. He left us a note asking us to meet him at the mission house at 10 a.m. to help him present our Lamina Program to the canton leaders. Upon our arrival, we were greeted with a packed house. All but three cantons were represented. We were thrilled at the attendance. In addition to being canton leaders, these people also served as Obras de Caridad workers, serving on many diverse programs helping to meet the needs of the poor in their communities. Fr. John asked me to explain our program while he acted as my interpreter. I began my presentation with the following statement:

"You asked us for lamina and we have promised you that we would supply it for you. As you know, God is working through Operation Rescue, Inc. to meet your needs. Since God doesn't always act as soon as we would like him to, we tend to think that He doesn't hear our prayers for help. But let me assure you, God has heard your prayers and today, He will answer them! Today we will begin the program to distribute the lamina that you need. Here is how it will work:

- The representative from each canton will receive eight numbered tickets.
- Each ticket can be redeemed for one bundle of five sheets of lamina at a price of $1.00. If a family is unable to pay the $1.00 cost, I will help them myself.
- As canton representatives, you are in charge of how the tickets you will be given will be distributed and to whom.
- Each representative will be asked how the lamina will be used in his/her canton when they come to pick up the lamina and take it back to their area.
- A representative may use one bundle for his/her house if needed.
- The future of repeating this program will be

determined by how well these rules are followed by everyone.

- Finally, the money collected will be credited to the Obras de Caridad general fund for further humanitarian programs.
- The lamina will be ready for distribution on July 20th at the rectory on the church grounds.

With that, Father began answering a flurry of questions. It was clear that we touched their hearts with new hope. The excitement in the room was palpable as the representatives began hugging us and telling us how much they needed this help. They thanked us profusely even though we assured them that God was answering their prayers, not us. For at least this one brief moment, their world was filled with the joy of promises kept and the light of hope for the future. To them, this was something different from what they expected. This particular project would help so many of their families; it would make a tangible, long-lasting difference to ease the tribulations of their culture. In the business world, this would be called a Red-Letter Day: this signified a day when everyone worked together as a group and excelled as individuals. For the Obras de Caridad, their goals were met; and for the individuals receiving lamina, their dreams had come true.

Just after the meeting, Marsha and I went up to the terrace on the roof of the rectory and looked out over the beautiful mountainside. It was quiet and peaceful there, a perfect setting for reflection. I recalled that earlier in the day, I handed out envelopes to be redeemed for lamina. As I was standing in front of each anxious El Salvadoran, a memory of several years prior came flooding back to me. My thoughts took me to Christmas Eve 2012. Marsha and I were happily engaged and we were eager to spread our Christmas spirit. So we decided to visit the St. Joseph Shelter for Homeless Men in a city near our house. I felt transported back to the moment that I was standing in front of a line of 66 homeless men, handing out envelopes that contained a Christmas card and a $20 bill. These men were excited and anxious for their gift, just like the El Salvadorans earlier that day. They were so joyful at such a small gift, and like the poor in El Salvador, they were the forgotten people living in the margins of society.

We were touched by their gratitude and in that moment we made a silent commitment to return to the homeless shelter the next year; same time, same place. The only difference was that our gift was not $20, we doubled it to $40! Once again, these men were ecstatic! Some of them cried out, "Now, I finally have enough money to buy my child a Christmas gift!" And, in anticipation of our arrival, a few residents even gave us small gifts out of their precious but few belongings. Just like in El Salvador, we were speechless with their generosity.

The following year, the ownership of the shelter had changed hands and we were told that we could no longer continue with our practice of giving money. We were really disappointed because it had given us so much joy. Saddened by this new development, we wondered where our faith journey would lead us next. Can you guess? It was only a few months later that we made our first trip to El Salvador; and you know what happened after that! As we transferred our efforts from the homeless shelter to Operation Rescue, Inc. Marsha was lead to a scripture below.

"You are an industrious and reliable servant.

Since you were reliable in a small matter I will put you in charge of larger
affairs. Come;
share your master's joy!"

Matt. 25: 21

We both felt that this scripture explained why we were being
lead to move on from the homeless shelter to Operation
Rescue, Inc. God seemed to leave his footprints on both of
these experiences. It occurred to me how many times the
number forty shows up in the Gospel: 40 days of Lent, 40 days
after Easter we celebrate Pentecost, Jesus went into the desert
for 40 days and 40 nights. When I recognized the connection
of the $40 we gave to the homeless shelter residents, and the 40
pieces of lamina we gave to each canton representative, I had a
deep and abiding understanding that God was with us, and had
been with us in all our efforts to help His poor. You can call it
coincidence, but the way Operation Rescue, Inc. was founded
and funded; I have to concede that what we call a coincidence
is in reality the grace of God working in our lives. Marsha, who
is a certified Spiritual Director, always says that people don't
often see God working in their lives simply because they don't
know what He looks like. Look for God in the story of your life.
Remember this quote, *"Just because you can't see air, you don't stop*
breathing. And just because you can't see God, it doesn't mean you stop
believing."

Day 50

The previous days just flew by and before we knew it, we
arrived at the day that the Obras De Caridad representatives

were to arrive at the church courtyard and pick up their allotment of lamina. The day before, the warehouse where we placed our order delivered six hundred sheets of lamina. They promised to return this day with four hundred more sheets, and indeed, they did. However, sleep evaded me the night before. I was both nervous and excited about our lamina project. I laid awake for hours; looking up at the dark sky that was intermittently lit up with distant lightning. As I mentioned earlier, it was rainy season during the time of our visit, and I hoped that the next thunderstorm would not reach our area until the following day. That would give our families time to reinforce their old roofs with the new lamina they would receive later that day. Even as I prayed that that would happen, I still couldn't believe that our Lord had chosen us to be His hands and feet on this mountain, in a culture so foreign to us that we couldn't even speak the language. He could have chosen so many other more equipped people to carry out this task for Him. Just realizing what a privilege it had been for us to participate in this unique work of charity brought tears to my eyes and down my cheeks. I felt humbled beyond words. Actually, I don't think I slept at all that night.

Soon the sun came up, the clock struck 6:30 am, and we began our busy day. By 7 a.m. the women of the Obras de Caridad group began arriving. Father had been storing extra bags of rice and beans just for such an occasion. As soon as they all arrived, the women began filling boxes and bags with Fr. John's gift of food, while the men sorted out the lamina into bundles of five sheets each. It was quite a site; people were bustling around everywhere, wearing big smiles on their faces. The sun rose early and bright, promising to be a dry but very hot day. In order to avoid the heat of the afternoon, people came early to gather their lamina and by 8 a.m. the courtyard was packed with men, women, and children. Thanks to the distribution system we worked on the night before, the people lined up and waited patiently for the number on their ticket to be called. The lamina was loaded onto trucks that would deliver the sheets to the homes of families chosen to receive them. Marsha and I never did find out where these trucks came from or who was even driving them. We decided to just be glad they were available and turned our attention to filling water cups for the adults and handing out lollipops to the children.

It looked like a fiesta had broken out on the church grounds. Laughter and music filled the air as all the Obras de Caridad members greeted us with hugs and handshakes. It was uplifting to see so many happy people; grateful people with hope in their eyes. We definitely earned their trust since we were able to fulfill our promise of delivering the lamina to them. They were becoming our friends and family; and we were falling in love with them. I was especially pleased that one man said to me as he left the church grounds, "By nightfall all of this lamina will be firmly attached to houses in our community. People who have been getting wet while sleeping will sleep peacefully tonight being protected from the rain." His words were exactly what I was praying for the night before.

By noon all the lamina, beans and rice, and lollipops had been distributed and courtyard was empty. All over the surrounding mountainside in twenty-three cantons roofs were being repaired or replaced. Prayers had been answered and mercy and love prevailed.

Later that evening, after Mass, Miguel came to us and gave us a piece of paper that recorded the morning's activities. When the representatives turned in their tickets, they listed the names of the families that received the lamina and their respective cantons. Miguel had taken that information and summarized it into a concise list of how many pieces of lamina each canton received and how they were distributed. We learned that one hundred and sixty-nine families had been helped that day; one hundred and sixty-nine families would sleep peacefully and safely that night; and one hundred and sixty-nine families went to bed having had a full meal that evening. What a great way to spend God's money! Give praise to the Lord; for in Him, with Him, and through Him, all things are possible.

ELEVEN

SOLIDARITY WITH THE POOR - WEEKS SEVEN AND EIGHT

Day 52

Marsha and I woke up early eager to get started on what turned out to be a long and emotionally turbulent day. We were headed out to two distant cantons: Canoas and Chiquileca. Our mission was to interview four families and evaluate their status to determine if they were candidates for a new Operation Rescue, Inc. house. Initially, it seemed like a moot point, because almost everyone living in the mountains of Teotepeque would qualify as desperately needing a new house. But our immediate objective was to find the family that would receive the next two houses. It would have been an impossible task for just Marsha and I with our American background. But fortunately, we had the input and perspective of Fr. John and Miguel to calibrate our judgement to the social norms of the culture we were serving.

Familiar with the ordeal we endured each time we made our trek up the mountain, this trip was no different; except that the air was a little more humid, the temperature a little higher, and the mud a little more slippery. We were in the middle of their winter, the peak of the rainy season, so this was normal in El Salvador. As usual, the truck took us as far as it could, and then the proverbial walk up the mountain or down into the valley ensued.

We arrived at our first destination. It was an unexpected experience. Here we found a mother of four children and her husband. They already had a rather large home with four separate sleeping areas. They also had a cistern that was able to provide them with fresh drinking water to drink. Additionally, and to our surprise, they had a total of seven pigs and an assortment of free-range chickens. I could see that the roof on this house was in need of new lamina and they were living on dirt floors, but other than that, they were really living within pretty high standards compared to the other families we had encountered. I have to admit that the thought entered my mind that this experience might make our decision a little easier.

We moved on to our second destination. The walk up the mountain was especially treacherous and due to the heat, and Marsha seemed to be fading fast. She is usually up for any challenge, but honestly, I didn't think she was going to make it. The path was so full of rocks it was difficult to navigate. I thought it would be easier if I just stepped on the rocks instead of avoid them, but I was wrong. The rocks, although embedded in the mud, moved every time I stepped on them, making is almost impossible to maintain my balance. When we arrived, we were disappointed to find that no one was home. Exhausted, we decided to rest for a while in hopes that the homeowner would soon return.

About ten minutes into our respite, we were pleasantly surprised when we saw two women making their way up the mountain toward us. When they arrived, the older of the two women presented us with the deed to the property, proving to us that the she was in fact the owner. She was very proud of this document; property ownership was hard to come by in this area and she knew it played an important part in being selected to receive a house. I could sense her pride and certainly wanted to honor it, but it had been quite some time since we had seen a property at this level of disrepair. We were truly shocked.

The rusty roof of this house was held up by tree branches that could barely serve their purpose. They were hollowed out due to age, weather damage, and an infestation of termites. Marsha inadvertently leaned on one, and the entire roof began to sway. Of course, the floor was mud. Chickens were in our path; pigs were running everywhere, and a goat was tied up a few feet away. Animal droppings were littered throughout. The odor was so putrid; we found it difficult to breath. The four children that lived in this filth were ages nine to seventeen years old. They were left alone every day because their father had died two years earlier and their mother had to work in the fields to earn food to feed her family.

We began an interview and asked all the same questions that we asked every family. But in the back of my mind, I knew that this family had to be helped. We had the power to do it and as far as I was concerned, my decision had been made to accept them into the program right then and there. However, we would have to go through the proper protocol and screening process in order to be fair to everyone. When we finished the interview, we exchanged hugs and made our way down the mountain. The woman, who was the owner of the house, picked up her machete and returned to the corn field to complete her days work.

The third family we were considering did in fact need a home but did not own the property. We knew that if we constructed the house on their property, the owner would evict them and take advantage of the improvements himself. In some cases when no one owned the property, the mayor would step in and give a family the rights to a property as long as someone from that family was living there. However, since this property had an established owner, the mayor had no authority over the property.

The fourth family we visited was a young couple in their mid-twenties who had one small child. They were currently living with the young mother's brother and his family. Her brother owned a little bit of property behind their current house that he inherited from their deceased parents. He was willing to give the property to his sister if we were willing to build a house for them. The young couple really wanted to begin a life of their own but had no means to do so. We felt that building a house for them, right near their extended family, would be beneficial for both families.

As we began our drive home, we decided to use that time to discuss the interviews we had with the four families we visited. We agreed to provide houses for the second and the fourth family at that time. The other families could remain on the list of families that might be chosen at a later date. Having completed our goal of identifying the next families within less time than expected, we decided to just drop in on two families that had received houses the previous year. We were so very pleased to see that both families had made improvements on the original structure we provided.

One family had been fortunate enough to add electricity to their home. This was rare indeed. The El Salvadoran government provided only a few power lines up in the mountains. In fact, in all of our travels up the mountains to twenty-six cantons, we only saw one telephone pole. The other family had the initiative to create a little covered patio space just outside the kitchen area. The floor of the patio area was still mud, but they had found some used wood and lamina that they were able to fashion into a roof. We gave them a few battery-operated light switches that provided some light for them. They were extremely excited about being able to see during the nighttime hours. This is certainly something we take for granted in the United States.

The most pleasing part of our observations at these last two Operation Rescue, Inc. homes was the pride you could see that they had in their home. Both homes were neat and organized; the children were happy and playful, and the parents felt a sense of purpose and accomplishment with their new surroundings. The material and labor to build the house only cost $2,160, but the extent to which the house changed their outlook on life and their vision of the future, the ultimate value of the house was beyond compare. It turned out to be, indeed, their harbinger of hope.

Day 54

At this point, we had been in El Salvador for several weeks and up until this day, Marsha and I had been totally dedicated to our working on Operation Rescue, Inc. In fact, for the last several years, our mission had been the focal point of all of our activities. In the first book of the bible, Genesis, God created the earth in six days and decided to use the seventh day as a day rest. With that in mind, we decided that we, too, needed a time of rest. So, we decided to take a week away and fly out to Portland, Oregon and visit Marsha's son who was about to celebrate his 40th birthday. We shared the idea of a birthday visit with others in the family and as it turned out, several of them decided to join us.

We reserved two vacation houses on the Columbia River, and had a great time. However, I have to admit that, even though we had only spent two months in El Salvador, we really did deal with culture shock. We were so glad we went for the family visit, but we were also glad to return to Teotepeque and resume our work there.

Day 55

A calendar week had passed and we returned to Teotepeque late the previous night. This day began early at 6:30 a.m. as we were expecting a mission group from Cleveland, Ohio to arrive. We had planned to spend the day blessing houses that were already built and helping to build new homes. We headed off to Canoas where we had finished a second home and had begun a third one. At the outset of our mission, our plan was to build one house in each of twenty-three cantons; then move on to build a second house in each canton. Since that had been accomplished, we were now starting on our next round of houses.

By this time, the communities understood our building schedule and were anticipating our second visit. Now they were ready for us and it had become a community event each time a new house was built. Families from the immediate neighborhood arrived early to assist the workers in moving the building materials from the drop off site up to the construction site. This usually meant volunteers were needed to personally carry the materials over some rough terrain up the mountainside where no vehicles could possibly travel. In one instance, the volunteers, man, woman, and child, each picked up one cinder block and carried it up the hill in single file. The homeowner, looking down the mountain from the worksite, remarked that it looked to him like a trail of ants carrying food to their colony.

In addition to helping with logistics, the community leaders organized a program for feeding the construction crew while they were building the houses in their canton. This program emerged when the construction workers decided that since they lived so far away and had no personal transportation, it made more sense to stay at their work location than traverse down (or up) the mountainside to their own home. The family who was receiving the house, with the help of their neighbors, would be responsible for feeding the workers the best they could. This program added a dynamic that no one had anticipated. We were able to see firsthand the goodness of our God; He seemed to place people where they were needed and gave them the free will to live the gospel in whatever way they could. The love and service shared by all was far reaching, spanning distance, generations, abilities and opportunities. It was an astonishing experience to actually see, hear, and touch the unconditional love of God between His children!

TWELVE

SOLIDARITY WITH THE POOR - WEEKS NINE AND TEN

Day 61

By this time of the season, the temperature was reaching the one-hundred-degree mark and the humidity was over ninety percent. Standing outside, just breathing became a very difficult task. On this day, our mission was to walk the streets of Teotepeque to visit three new homes that had been previously built. Because Teotepeque was on the side of the mountain, our walk was strenuous and challenging. Four dedicated members of the Obras de Caridad joined Marsha, Miguel and me. We needed to get photos, bless each house, give each family a lock for their front door, and distribute their portion of rice and beans.

In addition to that, we wanted to make sure that every house was built exactly to the specifications that we mandated. Recently the builders had been able to complete each house in less time than when they had begun this project. We hoped they that they had not been "cutting corners" to get more time off between houses, and were very happy to find that every house was built exactly according to our specifications. The reason the houses were getting done faster was due to the fact that the builders were becoming more organized and working more efficiently. We were very proud of their work ethic, creativity, and the skills they were developing; skills that would serve them well the rest of their lives, even after Operation Rescue, Inc. was completed.

It only took two hours to complete our visits, but coupling the terrain with the heat and humidity, we were exhausted by the end of the day. Not only exhausted but satisfied with our workers and uplifted by their progress. We rested in the evening and retired early in anticipation of a similar schedule for the next day.

Day 62

Inspired by our success of the previous day, we decided to visit five houses this day. We planned to travel to the remote canton of Chiquileca. It was situated at the top of one of the highest mountains in the area. As usual, we traveled by truck several miles up the mountain; then had to walk at least one mile down into the valley. The path was very narrow forcing us to walk in a single file. It was tense and unnerving because we had to trek through a very dense cornfield. Previously, we had been warned that these fields were fertile ground for snakes and venomous spiders. Once again, we had to look up to follow our guide but look down to make sure we didn't step into a dangerous situation. It was a relief when we finally saw the shiny metal of a roof off in the distance peacefully nestled in the middle of the field.

It was such a pleasant surprise we encountered there. Upon meeting the family and seeing the house close up, my first thought was that our trip up and down the mountain was well worth the effort. The family did not know we were coming, but I could tell that they were happy to welcome visitors to their isolated home. The house was exceptionally clean and well-kept both inside and out. The lady of the house was pleased to show us what she had done to turn the simple house into a warm and comfortable home for her family. She must have recently washed down the floor of the house because it was spotless, rendering a fresh fragrance to the entire inside of the dwelling. The walls were decorated with pictures of her family, drawings from school children and mementos of her faith. She had just finished bathing her four-year-old special needs child. The child was shy and unsure of how to greet us. The oldest daughter was about fifteen years old. It was easy to see that one of her duties was to help in the kitchen. She was in the midst of cooking dinner when we arrived. Unlike her younger sister, she seemed happy to have company and welcomed us warmly. The father of this family was off working in a distant corn field, lucky to have found work harvesting corn and happy to earn food for his family. He was used to rising early, walking hours to his worksite and returning home in the evening. We were sorry we missed him and would have liked to congratulate him on his home and his resourceful family.

One of the characteristics of this family was that they were able to build a large patio attached to their house. It must have been at least one thousand square feet. It had a roof and sturdy beams to support it. On two sides of the patio, pepper plants had been hung from the roof to begin a drying process that would allow them to be stored and used at a later time. It was my impression that this patio was where most of the daily activities of the family took place. The actual house that we built for them was used as sleeping quarters. Part of their original dwelling was still intact and was used for a kitchen. A shower area had been designated on the edge of the property. It consisted of an elevated cinder block floor and a basin of clean water. The entire area was organized, efficient, neat and clean. It was hard to believe that they had done so much with so little. We were beyond impressed. Clearly the members of this family were good stewards of the resources they had been given.

The next home we wanted to visit was not too far from the first. As usual, the path to get there was narrow, rocky and laden with pitfalls. It ended with a two-hundred-yard uphill climb to reach the home. We must have been getting better at navigating the terrain because the trip was relatively uneventful.

When we arrived, we found that the home was built over-looking the valley, a scene that offered a stunning view of the beauty of the mountain and the ocean below. In this lovely setting, we found a family of six, three girls, one boy, and a mother and father. The father was an unusually tall man among his peers, standing about six feet tall and probably weighing over two hundred pounds. He appeared to be strong and healthy, also an anomaly in this population. He was very gracious and greeted us enthusiastically. Through our inter-preter, we understood that he was embarrassed that, despite his continued efforts, he had been unable to find work, but he was proud of his home and excited to show us how clean and well-kept it was. Beyond the living area, he had used some cinder blocks that he had been gathering over the years to build a fish-pond. Since the ocean was at the base of the mountain, he would take day long fishing trips to catch fish to feed his family. The fish would be stored in the pond he built for the short time it would take for his wife to cook them and serve them for a meal. I was very impressed with his ingenuity and efforts to use whatever natural resources he could find to provide for his family. I also noticed that he had two very large turkeys and several chickens to help sustain them. This family worked together to survive; not one of them felt sorry for themselves or had an attitude of entitlement. Instead, they were grateful for what they were able to accomplish and thanked God for what they did have.

The last three remaining homes we had to visit were nearby. There we also found people who were living in abject poverty but were positive and cheerful. In each case, the new home that Operation Rescue, Inc. had built for them gave them a reason to hope for a brighter future.

As we made our way down the mountain, we used the last amount of energy we had left. Psychologically we were uplifted and energized, but physically we were drained and exhausted. It had been six hours since we departed the church grounds that morning and we hadn't stopped to rest or even eat the lunch Dalia packed for us. Our driver always stayed back with the truck and when he saw us coming, he turned on the ignition and started the air conditioning. The cool air and soft seats of the truck were a stark contrast to what we had experienced that day; it made our trip back home a welcome relief.

Day 63

Our 2017 extended visit to El Salvador was coming to an end. Before we began our preparations for departure, Marsha and I decided to reflect on what we had recently experienced. Over the past ten weeks, we had observed a culture far different from the one we were accustomed to. The word different must be qualified not to be understood as a judgement, merely a comparison to our native culture. Each culture had its own advantages and disadvantages; each culture carried with it pain and suffering, as well as happiness and contentment. There are people in the El Salvadoran culture who are extremely talented, intelligent, productive, loving, and who deeply care about one another. I have met people who would be considered abjectly poor by American standards, but yet they give whatever they have to those who are also in need. They don't seem to be afraid of poverty; they lived it and they rose above it. The generosity of their hearts extended beyond material needs to meet psychological, social, and spiritual necessities.

I have also seen this kind of generosity in our American

friends who donated to Operation Rescue, Inc. They, too, expressed their love of all of God's children by sharing their resources. Those who had a lot gave a lot; those who had little, gave what they could. In one instance, after hearing our story, we received a handful of change from a teenager who reached into the pocket of his jeans and gave us all he had. Even those who had no money to offer gave us encouragement and prayers of support. Marsha was overwhelmed at the scope of support we received. One thing that surprised her was how many people thanked us for the opportunity to fulfill their call to serve God's poor. They commented on the fact that they always wanted to give but didn't know to whom or how to go about doing it. We provided them with a legitimate, accountable process established by members of their own communities who were available in person to substantiate where their money would be applied. They were donating to us, and at the same time, thanking us for the opportunity!

While we were in El Salvador, we not only spent time in the mountain villages, but also attended events in some small and large cities. We attended churches, funerals, weddings, quinceañeras (parties hosted for young girls on their fifteenth birthday), fiestas, and fireworks displays. We had the opportunity to visit doctors, clinics, schools and an orphanage and were able to experience first-hand a wide spectrum of the El Salvadoran culture. The more we immersed ourselves into the daily El Salvadoran lifestyle, the more we found similarities to our American culture emerge. As soon as we were able to adjust to the physical limitations of the country, we realized that all people of all ages faced unfairness and adversity. In both cultures, parents worried about their teenagers and wanted their children to have better lives than they had.

I must note one amusing similarity between American women and the women we met in the mountain villages. In the

Unites States when you ask a woman if you can take her picture, she will say yes, but wants to check her hair and her outfit first. This also happens in El Salvador. We were about to take a picture of a family who received a home and the lady of the house motioned for us to wait a minute because she needed to go back inside the house. She had been working in her yard, so her hair was windblown and in disarray. Additionally, neither her flowered skirt nor her striped blouse fit very well, as all of her clothes had been donated. Within a few minutes, she returned with the same skirt and a newly washed, over-sized plaid blouse with her hair neatly pulled back into a bun on the top of her head. Now she had a bright smile, now she was ready for a picture. She really didn't look much different to us, but she felt better about her appearance. After all, it was a special occasion when she was included in a picture.

We found that a spark of hope and pride still lived in the El Salvadorans. However, their living conditions, economic restraints, governmental complexities, poor health care, and limited educational opportunities weighed heavily on their ability to see a better future. Beneath the yoke of these belittling issues, their core values remained intact: serving their families, friends, and faith. As hard as they tried to remain positive and hopeful, it was difficult as the fear of gang violence was ever present. Before we began Operation Rescue, Inc., it had been mostly contained in the big cities, but, by the time of our extended visit it had reached the otherwise, peaceful mountainside. Since our practice had been to register our visits with the US Government, we routinely received emails warning us about the eminent danger and an admonishment to refrain from visiting the country we had come to love. Originally, we were conflicted about whether to begin this journey or not, but our calling to serve God's poor was irresistible for us both.

Day 70

At last, our day of departure had arrived. During our two and a half month stay, our lives had been greatly impacted; we would never be the same. As we packed to begin our trip back home, we took time to reflect on how specifically we had changed during our visit. We had grown spiritually, psychologically, and emotionally. Our priorities had been turned completely upside down, and we developed a new definition of value and a set of new goals. When we first arrived, we were laboring under the misconception that the Western way of life would bring us joy and contentment. We had worked so hard to attain happiness and success, that joy and contentment had escaped us. However, we found both in the obscure, small, forgotten country of El Salvador. One of the most precious gifts we received as a couple was that Marsha and I both shared the same newfound blessings. This made our sacred bond of marriage grow even stronger.

THIRTEEN

WHAT DO WE DO NOW?

What Do We Do Now? By 2018, we had built eighty-five houses and had enough money to meet our one hundred house goal. We looked back on our journey and couldn't believe how much had been accomplished. On one hand we were thrilled that we could see a clear path to the fulfillment of our original goal, but it did beg the question, *What do we do now?* We looked at each other for guidance, but neither of us knew the answer to our question. We were not ready to let go of Operation Rescue, Inc., so we decided to do what had worked in the past. We would just wait and see what the Lord had for us.

We didn't have to wait long; a month later a reporter from the Elyria Chronicle Newspaper called and asked if she could do an article on Operation Rescue, Inc. She had heard of our work through one of our neighbors and wanted to learn more about it. Marsha and I spent an hour and a half on the phone with her one afternoon and tried to sum up what we had done over the last four years. We were a little caught off guard and didn't know exactly where to start or how much information she wanted to know. But she was a consummate professional and guided us with her questions. About one week later, the article hit the newsstands. It turned out to be an entire half page and included several pictures we had emailed to her. The reporter did an amazing job. She had taken our scattered thoughts and words and put them into a logical, concise, and very moving story. We had numerous friends say that they were glad they saw the article because before they read it, they never realized the entire scope of our mission.

A few days after the article ran, Marsha got a call from a woman who had read about our story. She said that she was so thankful to have learned about Operation Rescue, Inc. She was an eighty-five-year-old widow who lived alone. Even though life was not easy for her at this time in her life, she was so grateful to God for all that He had done for her. She was looking for a concrete way to show her gratitude and believed that she found her answer in building a house for God's poor. It was an impressive expression of gratitude. Within a week, we received a check in the amount of $2,100, which was the total cost of a home at that time, along with a note of appreciation for our work.

Several days later, I received a phone call from another woman who asked if she and her husband could set up a time to meet with us so they could learn more about our charity. Naturally we agreed to meet at our home. Prior to their arrival, I compiled some brochures, flyers, and pictures to give our words more depth and meaning. We sat and talked for about an hour. Having had all of their questions answered, the wife looked at her husband and asked, "Are you going to write them a check?" He just looked at me and asked, "Who do I make the check payable to? We wanted to build ten houses; that would be $21,000 right?" Once again, this donation far exceeded our expectations. Having had experienced the same type of surprise before, you would think we would have become more familiar with how God works, but, to this day, He never ceases to amaze us!

After a few weeks had passed, Marsha and I decided to reach out to the author of the newspaper article to let her know that her efforts would make a significant difference in this world. We had set an appointment for her to call us at any time that would be convenient for her. That time came and went with no call. Knowing her work ethic, we were more concerned that something had happened to her than anything else. About an hour later, she did call and profusely expressed her sorrow for being late. She explained that she had a doctor's appointment that morning and while she was in the waiting room, an emergency came up and her appointment had to be pushed back an hour.

She went on to say that 2018 had been a really bad year for her, having suffered a heart attack earlier in the spring and she had been very concerned about her health. This concern grew into a fear that loomed large over every thought that crossed her mind. Being the mother of two small children, she began to imagine that her children might have to grow up without her. This thought pattern even caused her to question the meaning and value of her life in general. Marsha and I expressed our concern for her situation. We wanted her to know how valuable she was and told her that the article she wrote clearly resonated with her readers resulting in donations equaling $23,100, enough to build eleven more houses. I told her, "God reached out and used your talent to serve his poor in El Salvador. Without you, these additional houses would not be built." We wanted her to see God's presence in these dark times and to know that He saw her fear and self-doubt, and that she was a precious child of His. We believe this was all part of God's plan for her life, our life, and the lives of his poor. She was so very grateful for our perspective on her life and trials. She realized that she was not alone and the difficulties that she was experiencing did in fact have meaning and far-reaching value. Marsha always says that God brings people together for their mutual good and His purposes. This story is a perfect example of what she says.

About one week later, a follow-up article was published highlighting the additional donations that we received from the first article. I know it is hard to believe, but within a ten-day period we received another $8,358 in donations. We couldn't believe what was happening. At the beginning of 2018 we hadn't known what to do. *Should we continue to ask for donations or bring our charity to a close?* Well, we got our answer; *we* didn't have to do anything. *God* would move the hearts of people to accomplish his work on earth. We just had to stay out of His way.

FOURTEEN

"WELL DONE MY GOOD AND FAITHFUL SERVANT"

Originally, I thought that our goal of building one hundred houses would be reached by May 2, 2019. But in early February, we realized that our hundredth house would be completed as soon as late March or early April 2019. With that, we decided to schedule a trip back to El Salvador to assist in finishing the last house. We contacted the Mission Team of our home parish, St. Joseph's in Amherst, Ohio, and invited any and all who would like to join us. We were thrilled that five people were able to make the trip: John Sabo, Carol Zellmer, Diane Kirsch, George Rolling, and Elizabeth Newman, who joined us for the first time. We also reached out to some of the people that we had developed relationships with over the past four and a half years: Jerry Gira, Joe Vasil, and MaryAnn Tinus. Jerry and Joe were able to join us, but MaryAnn was not. These people had become our close friends because they shared the same compassion that we did in serving God's poor in El Salvador. Each served in a different capacity, but our common bond was love for the people of this poor country.

Marsha and I decided to leave for Teotepeque on March

17. Since we had spent some time in Naples and Orlando, Florida that year, we reserved a flight out of Orlando Airport. The rest of the group was to gather in Cleveland and fly down together from there. We were then going to meet up them in Teotepeque. We had made plenty of plans in advance for our visit. Here is what we intended to accomplish:

- Reunite with our friends in Teotepeque.
- Spend some personal time with Fr. John.
- Make plans for the celebration of the completion of 100th home.
- Travel to San Salvador to purchase food and beverages for the celebration.
- Spend one-and one-half days physically working with the builders on what we thought was to be our 100th and final house.
- Plan our third Lamina Giveaway day. We had gathered another $6,000.00 for the purchase of the steel sheeting used for roofs of houses that we did not build but were still in need of desperate help. We were going to provide new roofs for 254 houses just before the rainy season.

However, as you probably know, the best laid plans don't always materialize. Unforeseen obstacles threatened to sabotage our mission. Previously, we had reserved a hotel for our last night in Florida at the Orlando Airport. We had an early flight out in the morning and wanted to get a good night's sleep before tackling our next adventure. We got to the hotel on schedule, but all of a sudden, I started to feel feverish. My symptoms mimicked the flu, but I had gotten a flu shot earlier. Even so, flu symptoms increased in intensity over a matter of just a few hours. Later in the evening, Marsha decided to take me to a clinic. The doctor there confirmed our flu diagnosis and prescribed some medication for me; along with bedrest for at least 48 hours. Not only did we have a flight out in the morning, we only had the room reserved for one night. However, I realized that in my condition, I had no choice but to change our plans. Marsha called the desk to ask for an extension, but was told that there was absolutely no way they could grant that for us. She was visibly upset and didn't know what to do. As miserable as I was, I called and insisted to talk to a manager knowing full well that something could be done if I could just talk to the right person. Of course, he was not available. I simply told the representative at the desk that we were *not* leaving. About an hour later, I received a call back from the manager. I explained to him that with me having a contagious flu, they should not even want to give our room to anyone the next day. I suggested that they talk to the people who had reserved our room and offer to secure a room for them at a different hotel. This would demonstrate that the health of their guests was their highest priority. Luckily, the manager did see the logic of my proposal and acquiesced to my request.

I remained locked up in our room for the next several days. I suggested that the housekeepers didn't enter the room but just leave clean linen and towels in the hallway each day. So, Marsha changed the linen herself and brought me food, medication, and lots of fluids. Even now, I cannot understand why she didn't get sick. After three days, I began to feel stronger and was able to make reservations to fly out to El Salvador within the next two days. Thinking back, that was the third time I had gotten sick right before leaving for El Salvador. *Coincidence?* I think not. It seemed to me that every time I planned to follow the Holy Spirit to do God's work, the evil spirit tried to prevent me from going forward. However, God's plan prevailed.

We arrived in El Salvador a few days later than planned but still two days before the date of our 100th House Fiesta Day. Our hope was to help with the plans for the fiesta, but all the preparations had already been done by the faithful servants of the Obras de Caridad. Once again, God touched the hearts of others to complete his work.

As it turned out, we were able to put our extra two days to good use. On our first free day, we had the privilege of connecting up with the Mission Team from St. Albert the Great near Cleveland, Ohio. This group of six men and one woman were also visiting Teotepeque during the same week we were there. They were an energetic, creative team who were all dedicated to providing safe, clean drinking water to the schools of the area. They had already served hundreds of high school and elementary students during their previous trips, but for this trip, their objective was to service two existing filtering units and to install one new unit in each of two additional schools. To emphasize the need for clean water, they had taken two petri dishes; one was filled with the water originally used, and one with water that was taken after the filtering system was put in place. It was staggering to see within twenty-four hours how many harmful bacteria had grown in the pre-treated water, as opposed to the post-treated water that was free from all harmful bacteria. That experiment ended any temptation I might have ever had to drink a sip of the untreated water—no matter how hot or thirsty I was.

Later that afternoon, we had the opportunity to attend a "Fresh Water Ceremony" at each of the two schools with the new filtration systems. The presentation they planned for us was a designed to be a dynamic expression of their gratitude. All the children and teachers gathered together; there was music, dancing and speeches from individual students explaining what it meant to have safe drinking water. To culminate the event, the teachers, students, and the guests from America were all given a glass of water taken from the new system. We all raised our glasses in salutation, gave thanks, and drank our water simultaneously. There was so much emotion in the room; it moved some of us to tears. All of us were joined in one memorable moment. We were all in solidarity, on one turf, celebrating God's mercy and love working within all of us. It was an amazing moment of grace.

The very next day, we were able to reconnect with our friends who we'd originally planned to travel with to work on the completion of the 100th house. We gathered at the work site early in the morning. The heat was unrelenting that day, but we were not to be derailed from of reaching our goal. Men and women, old and young, El Salvadoran and American all worked together. It was a beautiful sight; no division of ability, only unity of effort; no prejudice, only pride in working; no resentment, only respect for one another. It seemed like we were all one in body, mind, soul and spirit. The synergy was precious indeed; it was something our world needs more of.

This feeling of joy did not end at sundown; in fact, it intensified and culminated on the day of our fiesta.

The day that was chosen for our fiesta was the following Monday. Fr. John had planned a special mass in the Teotepeque at the Iglesias de San Pedro Apóstol (The Church of St. Peter). The morning we had been waiting for finally arrived! Our goal had taken almost five years to complete and it was a special day for everyone. However, we were not aware of the surprises that Obras de Caridad had planned for us. With Fr. John's help, they arranged for transportation to and from our celebration for all the families who received one of our houses. These families and friends from twenty-three cantons gathered together that day. Some people had traveled more than an hour to get there. Approximately seven hundred people poured out of buses and the beds of pick-up trucks. The large church was filled to capacity while many people lined the steps at the entrance of the church. Others had to gather in the courtyard. The ladies of the Obras de Caridad had arrived the day before, spent the night sleeping on foam mattresses on the floor of the church and rose at 3:30 am to begin preparing food for our fiesta.

When Marsha and I followed Fr. John out of the rectory, we were amazed to see the church filled with friendly faces and broad smiles. We knew all of these people; we knew their hearts, their homes, and their newfound hope for a better future. As we entered the back of the church, we stopped for a moment. I looked over at Marsha with misty eyes, and she said, "We have come full circle." Our dream had become reality and these humble, loving people had become our family. The joy of that community was in the air; it was palpable. Fighting back the tears, we looked around at all the faces. No need to suppress our emotions, as all around us we saw faces with tears flowing and heard voices with songs of praise. We proceeded up the aisle to begin Mass and to take our seats, as Fr. John proceeded to the altar.

Once we were seated, we expected the Mass to begin as usual, but we were in for yet another surprise. Our builders had organized a ceremony whereby one at a time, they carried one tool that was used to build the houses. Each tool was presented to Fr. John. He held it high above his head, blessed it and placed it at the foot of the altar. Symbolically, each of God's tools was acknowledged along with the worker who used it. By the end of the ceremony, the display included a shovel, a pick, a hoe, a cinder block and a wire cutter. These tools graced the altar, along with the men who used them. Music and clapping filled the church. Marsha and I were so moved, it took our breath away. Unable to speak at that moment, we just looked into each other's eyes and knew that words were unnecessary. The Mass began, all which was in Spanish, but we were getting better at understanding at least the prayers that were being said.

Finally, the time had come for Marsha and me to address

the congregation. We stepped up on the altar and I began our presentation. After each paragraph that I spoke in English in consideration of those who were from the United States, Marsha translated my words in to Spanish for the residents of the community. She was simply amazing, the perfect vocabulary spoken in perfect dialect. We spoke of how God had blessed us with the opportunity to serve the wonderful people of El Salvador. Wanting our message to be clear we emphatically stated, "Make no mistake about it, God has given you these homes, we merely serve Him. And we feel blessed to have been chosen to do so." We concluded by telling them that our lives had been changed forever by having known them. They had taught us generosity and unconditional love. We would return to the United States to share what we had learned and hopefully to spread these virtues to our friends and neighbors back home. We wanted them to know that we may have changed their culture a little, but they would have a far reaching positive impact our culture also. We now understood that kindness, love, and compassion can transcend time and space. They do not have to be restricted by borders, generations, or language barriers. Judging by the responses of those who heard our message, I think they agreed with us and found the same hope that we did.

After our presentation, Fr. John began reading one by one the names of the families who had received a new home, the name of the family that funded the house, and the canton in which it was built. It took at least forty-five minutes for him to read through all one hundred families. The crowded church was unbearably hot, and the humidity was reaching record highs. It didn't take long to understand why he decided to share all that information. First of all, we could see the big picture and the magnitude of the project. Working so closely in the details, it was hard to see the number of people and the expanse of miles Operation Rescue, Inc. had impacted. Secondly and probably most importantly, was to see the faces of the people when their name was read aloud in church. These people had so few opportunities to feel special. Having their name read in public gave them a sense of value and pride; it was easy to see, but hard to look at their abject humility. There wasn't a dry eye in the entire parish.

When the Mass concluded, one by one the families who received houses came up to us individually with hugs of gratitude and words of praise for our Lord, in Spanish. After having heard Marsha speak at Mass, everyone thought that she was proficient in their native language. That impression was born only by the hours of practice she put in translating the words we used in our presentation. She did know one other phrase in Spanish that seemed to be the correct answer to everything they were saying to her: "Gloria a Dios" (Glory to God). The reception line lasted for over an hour. Even our friend Miguel who had helped us with each and every house came up to us, and for the first time in five years of knowing him, I saw that he was moved to tears. This day was very special to him because he knew all too well how many people it took and how much work was done to reach the point we were at. He was with us every step of the way performing many different roles and carrying a multitude of responsibilities. Miguel was a man of great faith and many skills, and he never ceased to surprise and amaze us.

After the reception line, the celebration was in full swing. The ladies of the Obras de Caridad had prepared 700 foot-long roasted chicken sandwiches with their special salsa and grilled vegetables. The food looked delicious to us, but we were unable partake of it due to the health restrictions for Americans. However, the locals enjoyed it and by the end of the afternoon, all the sandwiches were eaten, and the drinks were gone. Music reverberated throughout the courtyard as the children ran around and played games. Ninety-five out of the one hundred families that received houses were in attendance. So many people had so much to celebrate; it truly was a grand fiesta! After three fun filled hours, transportation arrived to return our guests to their respective homes.

We ended the day at the rectory with Fr. John and talked about the amazing day we had. Looking back gave us a different perspective. Once the emotions settled down, we could clearly see how many people were instrumental in making this day a success. So much of the work was done behind the scenes, with no recognition of who was responsible. It was heartwarming to see that the volunteers were driven out of love for their Lord, and the community, not for their own personal aggrandizement or gain. Simply put, it was quintessential service born of humility.

The final notable event of this mission trip was our third Annual Lamina Day. Since we had accumulated $6,000 for this project, we were able to buy more of the high quality sheet metal that was guaranteed to last for twenty-five to thirty years. This particular giveaway would consist of eight sheets of lamina for each recipient, which was enough to replace their entire roof with a few extra pieces to construct a patio, walls for a latrine, or whatever they wished. We were able to procure enough lamina to improve 245 homes. As the people gathered in the church to sign in and pick up their voucher entitling them to the lamina, more work was being done outside the church in the courtyard. Miguel had gathered several of our volunteers and demonstrated how they were to separate the stacks of lamina into bundles of eight sheets each. They rolled up the sheets of lamina and secured them with rope. This made it possible for the El Salvadoran men to hand in their voucher, pick up the rolled bundle of lamina, balance it on their shoulders and carry it back to their house. There were a few trucks that arrived to carry lamina to houses that were too far up the mountain to be carried by one or two men.

While the men worked on the lamina, their wives and children gathered in the courtyard. We handed out lollipops and cold drinks. Each time a group of people gathered a spirit of celebration seemed to emerge. They were thankful for the charitable gifts they received, eager to share time with the missionaries, and enjoyed the company of their neighbors. Keep in mind that since most of them live relatively isolated in the mountains, so opportunities to gather are cherished. As we stood back and watched the camaraderie, we once again felt honored that we were chosen to hear their cries for lamina and be able to fill their need.

FIFTEEN

THE GIFT OF THE CHILDREN

"Truly I say to you,
unless you become like little children,
you will not enter the Kingdom of God."

Matt. 18: 3

Why do you suppose Jesus said that? Let's look at the qualities of little children.

- They trust their parents to take care of them.
- They don't worry about what they are going to eat, or what they are going to wear.
- Their natural tendency is to be playful and happy.
- They do not judge or hold grudges.
- Their ability to love is unhindered
- A child resting in the arms of loving parent is the epitome of peace.

When you list these qualities, it is striking that these are the same qualities that Jesus hopes to find in us: dependence, trust, joy, forgiveness, unconditional love, and peace. Now it becomes obvious as to why we need to be like little children. We learned a lot from the children of El Salvador.

The Children Welcomed Us

Never was the unfettered love that pours out of the hearts of children as obvious to me as it was in El Salvador. The very first time we met the children in the courtyard of the church grounds, we opened our arms to them, and they came rushing in. No words were spoken; only the sounds of love and laughter could be heard. It was like the spirit in our hearts connected with the spirit in their hearts. In an instant, an unbreakable bond was forged. And I say unbreakable because when we returned year after year, they remembered who we were and sought us out in the congregation of the church or whenever we walked the street of their village.

Juan José

One of my fondest memories was of a little boy Marsha first met when she was delivering rice and beans throughout the community with the Obras de Caridad representatives. I was unable to go along because I had been ill before the week of our trip and ultimately ended up with pneumonia while in El Salvador. This was our first visit, and Juan José was only about 4 yrs. old; a little small for his age because he had been never been in good health. His mother invited Marsha into their home where she noticed a small guitar hanging on the wall. When she asked about it, the lady of the house took it down and gave it to Juan José. He immediately began to play the guitar and sing a Spanish song that she was familiar with from her retreat work at St. Augustine's Church in the Cleveland. Of course, her heart melted.

During that trip, Juan José had become very close to the priest who accompanied us, Fr. Michael Denk. Fr. Michael also played the guitar and as the week wore on, the two of them played together often. Juan José used to say that he wanted to become a padre (Father/priest) when he grew up. Of course, Fr. Michael was so pleased. We had several visits over the years, where I, too, became attached to this precious, precocious little boy. We watched him grow up each time we visited; he never failed to greet us warmly whenever our paths crossed.

Felipe

Our hearts are both happy and sad when we think of Felipe. We met him when he was about fifteen-years-old. He worked at a restaurant across the street from the church grounds. Since his father was an alcoholic and either unable or unwilling to work, the family was in dire need. So, in the absence of any support from his father, Felipe volunteered to work to help support his mother and sister. He was a joyful young man who always smiling and full of energy. He seemed to be especially interested in the Americans who came to visit. In fact, as we traveled up the mountains and down the valleys, he ran beside our truck so that he could become part of our adventure. I can still see the smile on his face and the ever-present twinkle in his eye.

However, I have to doubt that he is smiling now. He has not been seen for about four years and his mother has no idea where he is. It seemed that he just disappeared. The fear, and the most probable explanation, is that he has become a victim of the dangerous, and often deadly gangs of El Salvador; namely MS-13. Felipe obviously loved his mother and his sister, so I believe he has had to sacrifice his freedom to protect them. If he is alive, I guarantee that the twinkle in his eye has been replaced by a tear.

The Dance at the School

I mentioned that there were many churches in the Cleveland area that served the community of Teotepeque. Our objective was to provide shelter, but there were also a number of groups that supported a parochial school on the church grounds. The school is named Colegio Católica Misioneros de Cleveland (Catholic School of the Missionaries of Cleveland). Their motto is Fe-Amor-Caridad (Faith-Love-Charity). These missionaries who supported the school were in Teotepeque at the same time we were. So, the students had the idea to put on a presentation in thanksgiving for the support of all those in the Cleveland area.

We all gathered in the courtyard; the missionaries, the teachers and all the students of the school attended. The children lined up, and suddenly the loud music blared out from the sound system. The song they chose was Elvis Presley's "Jail House Rock!" All at once, the children began a synchronized dance routine that had us all singing and clapping. It must have taken a lot of practice to put together such an awesome performance. They were so proud to entertain us with something that all Americans could relate to. And of course, music and dance both transcend culture barriers. We all felt bonded, like we were all members of one big, diverse family.

Sports Is a Universal Language

The courtyard of the church and school was a perfect place to gather. One hot day after the school day was over, someone brought a basketball outside. The older children from the school came out to play and minutes later the American teenagers from the missionary groups appeared and a basketball game began. Teams were formed, positions assigned, and spectators gathered, all without a spoken word. They didn't share the same language; they didn't need to. They knew basketball and that was all that was important. Boys and girls alike enjoyed the game. Winning wasn't the goal. Sharing time and space, erasing differences in language, culture, and geography was the simple win. Fr. John was particularly entertained by the basketball game. You may remember that he is six-foot-seven and had personally played the game in his youth.

Easter Egg Hunt

One of our visits to El Salvador was just before the Easter holiday. I wasn't sure what holiday traditions were shared there, but I thought, *"What child wouldn't like an Easter egg Hunt?* "So, Marsha and I organized an Easter egg Hunt for all the children in the area. We had no idea how many people would attend but we prepared for as many as we could. We bought lots of treats and filled about one hundred fifty plastic eggs. A social hall on the grounds of a church in Mizata was decorated. We were ready and waiting for the children to come. I will admit that we had a slow start, but as soon as the word got out on the street, the children flowed in.

It was a challenge to explain the rules to the different ages of children, but they got the message quickly and the fun began. These children were so used to having next to nothing that they could hardly believe they were allowed to find, keep, and enjoy the candy we freely provided. They ran around smiling, giggling, and gathering treats. Naturally, the older children were able to collect more treats than the younger ones, but the older children were eager and happy to share their candy. They acted on their own, with no-one telling them to do so.

Children have a way of losing themselves in the moment. They are not pre-occupied with the past or the future. As adults, we must find a healthy balance between living in the moment and planning for the future. After all, our Lord only "give(s) us our daily bread."

SIXTEEN

HIDDEN BLESSINGS

Operation Rescue, Inc. has indeed been a privilege and a blessing. As Marsha and I think back on our experience, we still can't believe all that happened, how it happened, or why it happened to us. It just seems too good to be true, but true it is. Many of the blessings we were given have already been shared in the pages of this book. During our interactions with the people of El Salvador, we experienced many situations that pointed to the parables of the Bible. Sometimes we felt like the stories of the Bible jumped off the pages of the book and were manifested directly into our lives in real time. We were so grateful for that at the time. But now, as we look back on our adventure in the fullness of time, we now see even more blessings that we didn't see in the moment. The closer we looked back at the last several years; we began to see examples of the behavior and attitudes that we see in the Beatitudes. Let's take a closer look at the similarities.

The Beatitudes can be found in the Bible: Matthew 5: 3 – 12.

Verse 3: *"Blessed are the poor in spirit, the reign of God is theirs."*

The people in the mountains of Teotepeque are very poor in spirit. They are not willful people who want everything their own way. They do not have a spirit of entitlement at all. They are filled with gratitude for every opportunity they can find.

Verse 4: *"Blessed are the sorrowing;*
they shall be consoled."

These people live with sorrow day in and day out. Just a few generations before they lived through a civil war, where the enemy was living among them. So many members of their families had been murdered. Even now they live in fear of the violent gangs. Sorrow is their heritage.

Verse 5: *"Blessed are the lowly,*
for they shall inherent the land."

All of the families we met were examples of profoundly humble people. I am not sure if the children were taught humility or if it was just endemic in the mountain culture. I thought this verse spoke precisely to the recipients of Operation Rescue, Inc. houses because they needed to be owners of the land on which we built the house. If they didn't own any land the mayor oftentimes provided them a conditional deed.

Verse 6: *"Blessed are those who hunger and thirst*
for holiness, they shall have their fill."

One of the mandates of the Catholic Church is that members must attend Mass every Sunday if at all possible. As that works in the United States, it does not work in El Salvador.

They have very few priests to cover so much territory that Mass is usually only offered once a month in the mountain areas. But what a celebration it is before, during, and after Mass. Before Mass, everyone gathers outside the church for fellowship. Keep in mind that they cannot easily visit with their neighbors due to the terrain and lack of transportation. The Mass itself usually lasts two hours, as opposed to Mass in the United States that lasts forty-five minutes to an hour. After Mass, the ladies of the families make *papusas* and grill them over an open fire. The teenagers mingle and the small children play games and enjoy piñatas. All ages love to attend Mass, as it is a place where they find respite from their difficult lives. Most of all they hear the word of God that brings light to their otherwise dreary existence.

Verse 7: *"Blessed are they that show mercy,*
mercy shall be theirs."

Most of the families we interacted with were multi-generational. They opened their homes to young and old alike. No one is to be left alone. We even met families that took in friends or strangers into their meager homes just so they could survive. This is mercy in action.

Verse 8: "Blessed are the single-hearted,
for they shall see God."

During the civil of the 1980s, over seventy-five-thousand people lost their lives. The poor had nowhere to turn but to their church and their God. It was the single place they could seek and find help. It's interesting that even the name El Salvador is translated as The Savior.

Verse 9: *"Blessed are the peacemakers,*
they shall be called the sons of God."

All the mountain people that we met were gentle and peaceful people. Even though they had reason to be full of anger, hate, and resentment, they were not. They lived in peace and harmony with their families and friends.

Verse 10: *"Blessed are those persecuted for holiness' sake, the reign of God*
is theirs."

The most powerful example of persecution is found in the life and times of Oscar Romero. He was the Archbishop of El Salvador during the civil revolution. He was the only advocate that the poor had during the years leading up to the conflict. It was not an option for them to seek help from the government so Archbishop Romero stepped up to help them; and as I said before, that lead to his martyrdom.

Verse 11: *"Blessed are you when they insult you*
and persecute you and utter every kind of slander against you because
of me."

This brings to mind the four women who advocated for the rights of the poor after the murder of the archbishop. There were three Catholic nuns: Ita Ford, Maura Clark, Dorothy Kazel and missionary Jean Donovan. On December 2, 1980, these four women were kidnapped, raped and murdered for their support of the poor. The news reported that they were led by nun Ita Ford who was a communist. It was a perfect example of persecution and slander.

Verse 12: *"Be glad and rejoice for your reward*

*is great in heaven; they persecuted the prophets
in the same way."*

It is a tall order to rejoice in the face of persecution, but we do have an example to follow, that is Jesus Christ. We do not live in the days of Christ, but we do experience fear, trauma, and sorrow. *Can we rejoice in our own life?* I don't know. Let's try it. We have little to lose and everything to gain.

Throughout the course of the book, we explained the *Why* of our mission, but now I would like to explain the *Why* of this book. Quite simply, our intention is to invite and encourage readers to say *yes* to God's calling in their own life. The gospel of Mark explains that Jesus sent his apostles out two by two to continue His work. Matthew 10: 19 says,

"Do not worry about what you will say or how you will say it. When the hour comes, you will be given what you are to say. You yourselves will not be the speakers; the Spirit of your Father will be speaking in you."

We invite our readers to share their experiences and spiritual journeys with us so we can pass on to others. Have courage, my friends, you are not alone.

ACKNOWLEDGMENTS

We would like to thank all the people who have made this story come to life. Father Michael Denk opened our minds and hearts to this adventure as he led us on our first visit to El Salvador. Having had missionary experience himself, he advised us not to go "if we didn't want this to change our lives." Also, thanks to Father John Ostrowski for his support and leadership in Teotepeque El Salvador, and to the Propagation of Faith in the Cleveland Diocese led by Reverend Stephen Vellenga.

The first trip we made to El Salvador was a cultural trip where we learned about the people, how they lived, and why they were forced to endure violence and poverty. This unique time made a profound impression on us and served to solidify our intention to help the El Salvadorans. We owe a great debt of gratitude to Fr. Paul Schindler. He spent ten years in El Salvador during the civil war and returned to La Libertad, El Salvador after retiring from his assignment in the United States. He is there even to this day. He was kind enough to meet us for face to face on more than one occasion. These were very powerful moments as he shared his experiences and perspectives on war, peace, human nature, and faith.

We continued to pursue our education of this time in history. When the opportunity to visit the University of Central America was made available to us we jumped at the chance to learn more. We viewed the "Exhibit of Artifacts, other original documents and books detailing the times between 1979 through 1992.

We've appreciated the friends we have made along the way who shared and supported our endeavor. The following people were our mentors and companions, each having their own individual missions in support of the people of El Salvador: MaryAnn Tinus, Jerry Gira, and Joe Vasil. We were faithfully accompanied by parishioners from our own parish: Carol Zellmer, Diane Kirsch, George Rolling, and John Sabo.

We'd also like to thank our corporate sponsors, State Farm Insurance Companies, Progressive Insurance Company, Amica Insurance Company, and Sherwin Williams, who all matched individual donations made by their employees.

We were blessed to be supported by the Lorain County Joint Vocational School, the St. Joseph Elementary School in Amherst, Ohio, St. Mary's Elementary School in Elyria, Ohio, the Amherst St. Joseph Mission Team, and St Rita's Parish in Solon, Ohio. Without them, we could not have been successful.

We will always owe a debt of gratitude to the following people: our most gracious donors, Ron and Frieda Bourne, Founders of the Bourne Foundation for their generous contributions in the loving memory of their son David Bourne; Greg Wasilko from Rocky River, Ohio and his many supporters who donated a home. We also honor the privacy of the couple in Amherst, Ohio who wish to remain anonymous having donated money for twenty homes. Thanks to Tracey and Linda Howell for their generous support and donations.

The list of all our donors is too lengthy to include in this book, but each one can be sure that their name is written on our hearts. Each donation was precious in our eyes, whether it was for $70,000 or for 70 cents. Every penny went to serving the poor.

Finally, we have a grateful heart for Jason and Ellen Hunker, for their effort, support, leadership and most of all their friendship over the past seven years. As Board Members of Operation Rescue, Inc., they have worked with us side by side throughout our journey. They are like family and we have been blessed by their presence.

Special thanks to our daughter-in-law, Autumn Gantz, who has made our dream of writing this book become a reality. Your knowledge and endless dedication to your work is deeply appreciated. We love you!

Our sincere thanks to our grandson, Brennan Norberg, who was responsible for the book cover. Your work here is but a mere example of what the future holds for you and your talent.

We must not overlook the gratitude we have for our new family of friends in El Salvador. They have blessed us with their love, spirituality and true friendship. Our journey is not over, we will continue on in whatever direction God takes us, but we do so with a much deeper understanding of God's unconditional love! We do not say, "Adios, solamente hasta luego!" When translated in English, we do not say "Good-bye" only "until we meet again."

ABOUT THE AUTHORS

——————————⟨⟩,⟨⟩——————————

This book is the product of both Marsha Norberg Gantz and David Gantz. For years, they each shared a desire to serve God. This book is a narrative that details how their desire became a reality. After traveling to El Salvador, this couple accepted God's call to build homes for the poorest of the poor in the villages surrounding Teotepeque, El Salvador.

Armed with little more than their will, they set out on a journey to live the Gospel. Their work has spanned over seven years, during which they spent three consecutive months living with the people of El Salvador. There they experienced first-hand the harsh living conditions of this impoverished part of the world.

Having no previous experience in the workings of a charity, they had to rely on God to complete their mission. At each and every turn they found God's presence. Marsha depicts the various "parables" from the Bible that spoke to them along the way.

Marsha received her bachelor's degree in English and Psychology from Kent State University. She continued her education by completing a four-year program earning a Spiritual Director's Certification from the Villa Maria Spirituality and Education Center in Pennsylvania. This has enabled her to work as a spiritual director with both individuals and groups.

David received his bachelor's degree from Bowling Green

State University in Education, after which, he spent nine years teaching and coaching at the high school level. Following that, he had a thirty-year career in Agency Management for the State Farm Insurance Companies.

It is their hope that their story will touch and inspire readers to create their own "Mission of Mercy."

- Website: operationrescueinc.com
- Email: davidwgantz@hotmail.com

About Brennan Norberg

Brennan is a senior at Kent State University in Kent, Ohio. He is majoring in Graphic Design and Art at Kent State. Brennan is looking forward to establishing his own career following his graduation in the spring of 2022. Our thanks for the wonderful book cover.

- **Email:** Banorbie99@gmail.com

facebook.com/operationrescueinc

twitter.com/operationrescu4

instagram.com/operationrescue4

Made in the USA
Columbia, SC
10 December 2021

50687167R00096